The Shakespear

THE SHAKESPEARE HANDBOOKS

Series Editor: John Russell Brown

PUBLISHED

FORTHCOMING

The Shakespeare Handbooks

The Tempest

Trevor R. Griffiths

palgrave
macmillan

First published 2007 by
PALGRAVE MACMILLAN
Houndmills, Basingstoke, Hampshire RG21 6XS and
175 Fifth Avenue, New York, N.Y. 10010
Companies and representatives throughout the world

PALGRAVE MACMILLAN is the global academic imprint of the Palgrave Macmillan division of St. Martin's Press, LLC and of Palgrave Macmillan Ltd. Macmillan® is a registered trademark in the United States, United Kingdom and other countries. Palgrave is a registered trademark in the European Union and other countries.

ISBN-13: 978–1–4039–3477–2 hardback
ISBN 10: 1–4039–3477–0   hardback
ISBN-13: 978–1–4039–3478–9 paperback
ISBN 10: 1–4039–3478–9   paperback

This book is printed on paper suitable for recycling and made from fully managed and sustained forest sources.

A catalogue record for this book is available from the British Library.

A catalog record for this book is available from the Library of Congress

10   9   8   7   6   5   4   3   2   1
16 15 14 13 12 11 10 09 08 07

Printed in China

To Kathy Rooney,
wie immer

Contents

General Editor's Preface

The Shakespeare Handbooks provide an innovative way of studying the theatrical life of the plays. The commentaries, which are their core feature, enable a reader to envisage the words of a text unfurling in performance, involving actions and meanings not readily perceived except in rehearsal or performance. The aim is to present the plays in the environment for which they were written and to offer an experience as close as possible to an audience's progressive experience of a production.

While each book has the same range of contents, their authors have been encouraged to shape them according to their own critical and scholarly understanding and their first-hand experience of theatre practice. The various chapters are designed to complement the commentaries: the cultural context of each play is presented together with quotations from original sources; the authority of its text or texts is considered with what is known of the earliest performances; key performances and productions of its subsequent stage history are both described and compared. The aim in all this has been to help readers to develop their own informed and imaginative view of a play in ways that supplement the provision of standard editions and are more user-friendly than detailed stage histories or collections of criticism from diverse sources.

Further volumes are in preparation so that, within a few years, the Shakespeare Handbooks will be available for all the plays that are frequently studied and performed.

John Russell Brown

Preface

The aim of this book is to enhance the reader's enjoyment and under-standing of *The Tempest*. A section that introduces key issues about the text and early performances of *The Tempest* precedes the main body of the work, which is a scene-by-scene 'Commentary' on the play in performance. This section considers key factors that may influence the theatrical interpretation of the play, paying attention both to how characters are created, through their own words and other characters' reactions to them, and to explicit and implicit stage directions, questions of costuming, music, actions and gestures, as well as how each scene contributes to the ongoing development of the play. 'The Play's Sources and Cultural Context' looks at factors that may have contributed to the making of the play, and it includes extracts from a number of works that influenced the play or exem-plify contemporary debates about issues that are raised in the play or by its dramatic structure. In 'Key Productions and Performances' I examine some of the most important stage versions before looking at 'The Play on Screen'. In 'Critical Assessments' (which includes extracts from some of the key early critics) I trace some of the ways in which the play has been interpreted by critics, and ways in which it has been influential outside the theatre itself.

On a few occasions, in order to enable the sections of the book to be read independently, I have repeated a small amount of material but usually, when there is an overlap, I have directed the reader to the relevant section.

In quotations from works written before 1800 I have conserva-tively and lightly modernized spelling and punctuation. I have quoted *The Tempest* from Stephen Orgel's Oxford edition (1987).

1 *The Text and Early Performances*

The text

The Tempest was first printed in the 1623 Folio edition of Shakespeare's plays produced under the auspices of his fellow actors John Heminges and Henry Condell and published by William Jaggard. It is the first play in that Folio (a large format volume), which includes the majority of the plays now accepted as Shakespeare's. *The Tempest* is divided into Acts and scenes throughout and has fairly comprehensive stage directions, though, like most Renaissance play texts, it misses some exits and entrances. It comes equipped with a list of characters and a statement of its location ('The scene: an uninhabited island'). The list of characters and the location are placed at the end of the play, whereas modern practice would place them at the beginning where they would be of more help to the reader. It is possible that they were placed where they were because the printers wanted to fill up what would otherwise be some white space on the page.

There has been considerable speculation about why this particular play was chosen to open the collection, with some scholars claiming that it was carefully prepared to give prospective purchasers a good impression of the volume. Some have also claimed that it was set as a typographical model for the volume, despite the fact that subsequent plays do not share many of its distinguishing features and may well have been typeset before *The Tempest* was. The play appears to have been set from a good manuscript, prepared by a scrivener, Ralph Crane, whose working practices are clear from a significant number of extant manuscripts and published plays. Modern editions modernize Folio spelling and punctuation as an aid to understanding (Crane was a particularly heavy punctuator), but there are relatively few textual problems and relatively few contentious readings in *The Tempest*.

Much editorial energy is rightly expended on trying to discover the exact nature of certain words or phrases, but the majority of the contentious readings in *The Tempest* actually make very little difference to how the play works in production. For example, while no one has yet established definitively what precise flora or fauna are represented by the 'scamels' that Caliban offers to find for Trinculo and Stephano at II.ii.166, it is very clear from the context that Caliban regards them as edible delicacies, and that is all that an audience needs to register.

While most editorial emendations consist of minor changes to obvious misprints there are a few more complex issues. For example, there is a more challenging textual crux in III.i.15, where the Folio reading 'Most busie lest when I do it' has exercised generations of editors, although in production it is unlikely to trouble audiences. Actors will have to decide between two broadly competing interpretations of the sentence, in which Ferdinand either thinks about Miranda most when he is working hardest or is able to think about her most when he is doing less work. An audience is likely to get the general point that he is besotted by her without worrying too much about the grammatical niceties.

Although textual scholarship can sometimes seem pedantic to those who are most interested in plays in performance, it can have significant impacts on what is actually said and how a play is interpreted. In Act IV, scene i, Ferdinand pays a compliment to Prospero, which is often printed, and therefore spoken, as: 'So rare a wondered father and a wise / Makes this place paradise' (ll. 123–4). The rest of the exchange between Prospero and Ferdinand is unrhymed, and strong claims have been made for an alternative reading in which 'wife' is substituted for 'wise'. Clearly that reading also makes sense: Ferdinand has acquired a father and a wife (that wife's name, not coincidentally, means wonder). Some editors have not pursued the issue even in their notes, usually printing 'wise' as unproblematic, although the old long 's' ('ʃ') could easily be mistaken for an 'f'. The issue appeared to have been settled in 1978 by Jeanne Addison Roberts, who traced the different states of the printing of this line in different copies of the Folio (Renaissance printers corrected their texts as they went along so that corrected and uncorrected versions of the same page may appear in different volumes). In her view the original spelling was 'wife' and the letter broke so that the 'f' came to be read as a long 's'. However, more recently, an even closer scrutiny of the passage, by Peter W. M. Blayney, seems to have confirmed the authenticity of the reading 'wise'. It is of course possible that the compositor or Ralph Crane had themselves misread a Shakespearean long 's' for an 'f'. On such accidents whole readings of a play may depend (Vaughan and Vaughan, Arden 3, pp. 136–8).

Sometimes editors have given speeches to different characters from those they are assigned to in the Folio. In Act II, scene i, for example, the context makes it fairly clear that lines 38 and 39 should probably be given to Antonio and Sebastian rather than the other way round as in the Folio. However, there has been considerable editorial dispute that touches on significant issues of interpretation, about whether the speech beginning 'Abhorred slave' (I.ii.350), given to Miranda in the Folio, should be assigned instead to Prospero. Editors who give this speech about educating Caliban to Prospero tend to regard it as too mature for a girl of Miranda's age, but this assumes both a degree of naturalistic consistency that is anachronistic in relationship to Shakespeare's dramaturgy and a view about what young women might or might not say or do that rests on equally tenuous psychological assumptions. If we apply strict forensic rules to this situation, we might note that in Act II, scene ii, Caliban appears to offer some corroboration that Miranda did help in his education when he refers to his mistress showing him the man in the moon. Similarly, in the context of preserving Miranda's modesty, we might note that Miranda's declaration of love to Ferdinand in Act III, scene i, draws on a vocabulary that is usually seen as connected with secret pregnancy but which could equally refer to the mechanics of sexual intercourse. In any case there is nothing intrinsic to the play that justifies removing the speech from Miranda, and the argument justifying its removal is circular.

The play's detailed stage directions, many of them apparently descriptive rather than practical, have been much discussed by scholars. Although we cannot be certain about their exact provenance, some critics have argued that Crane may have been describing a performance he himself had seen, perhaps augmenting Shakespeare's own stage directions with his own observations, although there is no surviving evidence of a performance close to the date of the publication of the Folio. In general, scholars have been far too ready to assume that records of stage productions as preserved in prompt books and play texts necessarily represent the final word on what actually happened at a given moment, but it is probably fair to say that a stage direction like 'Enter Mariners wet' (I.i.50), for example, is more likely to describe either an author's thoughts on what he wanted to achieve or an audience's visual impression of the storm, rather than to act as an instruction to a stage manager, who is more likely to have needed to be reminded to have a bucket of water ready at an appropriate time and place than what the result of having the water available would be. Similarly, when Ariel enters like a harpy (III.iii.52.3), the exact nature of what goes on is unclear. The wording of the stage direction suggests it was written either by someone who saw the scene without knowing exactly how the effect was achieved or by someone (Shakespeare) who did not need to elaborate at that stage in the writing process: 'a quaint device' is clearly not meant to provide practical guidance to a stage manager. If the Folio copy text had been a prompt copy there might have been some indication of whether Ariel's entrance involved flying and how the wings that fold down over the table functioned in relation to the banquet's disappearance. Similarly, in Act V, scene i, it is clear that at some previous point Prospero has created a magic circle, since the nobles 'enter the circle which Prospero had made' (l. 57.4), but there is no stage direction to indicate when he did so. In the existing stage direction Alonso comes in 'with a frantic gesture' as do Sebastian and Antonio; again, this suggests a visual impression of a staging rather than an actual stage direction. Whether these words are Crane's or Shakespeare's or someone else's they do give at least some impression of how the play may have worked in early performances.

Early performances

The earliest known performance of *The Tempest* took place at the court of James I on 1 November 1611 and if, as most scholars are agreed, Shakespeare was influenced by accounts of the wreck of the *Sea Venture* off Bermuda in 1609 that could not have been available before September 1610, it seems likely that he wrote the play sometime between September 1610 and November 1611. It was staged again at court in February 1613 as part of the extravaganza of entertainments that marked the presence of the Elector Palatine, who was to marry Elizabeth, James I's daughter. However, we do not actually know if the play's first performance was at court and there is no reason to suppose that it was created specifically with court performance in mind. Equally there is no reason to think that in 1613 it would not have been a good selling point for the theatre company to offer a play celebrating the union of a courtly couple when the authorities were choosing the plays that would be presented as part of the marriage festivities. Some scholars, speculating that there may have been some correlation between the play's subject matter and the court celebrations, have argued that the masque of Ceres was not part of the original play but was inserted for the 1613 performance. However, there was nothing unusual in Shakespeare including such entertainments in his work. Masques were certainly popular at court, and the form was developing under the influence of Ben Jonson, but courtly entertainments were not unfamiliar in public theatres as part of the dramatic action of plays as different as *As You Like It* and *The Revenger's Tragedy*, and Shakespeare had himself already used a similar device with the performance of 'Pyramus and Thisbe' as a wedding entertainment in *A Midsummer Night's Dream*. Although some critics have expended considerable energy on their theories of revision, there seems to be no compelling reason to doubt that the masque was an integral part of the play as originally conceived and that its features are specifically located in the dramatic and thematic necessities of the play. Moreover, the other plays chosen for the 1613 wedding celebrations included *Othello* and *The Maid's Tragedy*, neither of which is obviously tailored to the specific needs of celebrating a forthcoming marriage, so there is no particular reason to think that a masque needed to be added to *The Tempest* to make it more topical for the court performance.

According to the preface of the 1670 edition of John Dryden and William Davenant's 1667 adaptation of *The Tempest*, the Shakespearean original had 'formerly been acted with success in the Blackfriars'. When Shakespeare wrote the play he was both the resident dramatist of and a principal shareholder in the King's Men, the acting company that by 1611 was playing regularly at both the indoor theatre at Blackfriars and the Globe, their older, open-air amphitheatre. Early stagings of *The Tempest* may well have occurred at the Blackfriars theatre but there is no reason to suppose it could not and would not also have been performed at the Globe. The basic requirements of *The Tempest* can be met easily by a theatre with two entrance doors at the back of the acting area and a discovery space between them, a place above the stage for Prospero to appear in during Act 3, scene 3, that may also have been used by musicians and perhaps by some of the characters in Act 1, scene 1, a flying apparatus, and various musical instruments, thunder machines, costumes and so on.

Arguably some of the effects might have been managed in a more spectacular fashion in an indoor theatre but there is nothing demanded by the text of *The Tempest* that was beyond the technical capacities of the Globe. Although in *The Fair Maid of the West*, a play which is very close in date to *The Tempest*, Thomas Heywood has a chorus lamenting that 'Our stage so lamely can express a sea / That we are forc'd by Chorus to discourse / What should have been in action', it is not clear whether Heywood's play pre- or post-dated *The Tempest* (Gurr, 'Tempest', p. 91). Of course, it was conventional to lament the limitations of the theatre (as in the choruses to *Henry V*), but it is striking that Heywood was drawing attention to some of the difficulties in staging sea scenes contemporaneously with the first staging of Shakespeare's play.

In *The Tempest* the opening storm itself is created through wet mariners, whistles, confused noises and the sound of thunder (created by rolling a metal ball down a metal channel and drumming, see Gurr, 'Tempest', p. 95). Lightning could be created by using fireworks, but the stage direction in *The Tempest* refers only to the sound of lightning and not to visual effects. Many of the effects in the play depend partly on sound: the choruses of dogs, cocks, and bells; thunder claps; the spirit hounds; music, on stage or off stage – below the stage, in the tiring house or in the room above the stage to create a supernatural effect. Other effects depend on costume changes, such as the changing physical appearance of Prospero in his magic robes or as Duke of Milan, and of Ariel in whatever costume he first appears in, as a sea nymph, a harpy and, probably, Ceres, or by the use of costumes as stage props, as in Caliban, Stephano and Trinculo's distraction by the frippery in Act IV, scene i. Ariel's invisibility could be achieved partly by Prospero telling us he is to be invisible and partly by the simple fact of other onstage characters not noticing the supposedly invisible characters. The contemporary theatrical entrepreneur Philip Henslowe's papers include a reference to a 'robe for to go invisible' (Foakes and Rickert, 1961, p. 325), and Shakespeare's company may have used something similar as a conventional indicator of invisibility. If the stage doors and discovery space are used for most entrances, they could be supplemented by a stage trap for the disappearance of the banquet, which might also serve for a cave for Caliban and even an alternative entrance point for Ariel. Ariel can descend as the harpy on a flying apparatus, and the 'trifle' that Prospero presents to entertain Miranda and Ferdinand in Act IV, scene i, would benefit from flying-in one or more of the characters and perhaps from some scenery, although the dances need nothing more than skilled performers and musicians. In Act V Ferdinand and Miranda probably need to be discovered behind a curtain playing chess in the discovery space, and the frippery could be hung either between stage posts or at the back of the stage across a door or doors. Some of these effects might be easier to create in one or other of the two theatres available to the company or for the court performances, but there is no reason to suppose that *The Tempest* could not have been staged at any available venue without major difficulties.

One aspect of the play's structure that does reflect a change in playing practices compared with Shakespeare's earlier plays is the fact that Prospero and Ariel end Act IV and then reappear as the first characters in Act V. This is unusual for Shakespeare and probably reflects stage practice that originated at the indoor playhouses, where music was played in the intervals between the Acts so that the candles necessary for lighting indoor performances could be trimmed. This custom of entr'acte music was also adopted at the Globe so there is no reason why *The Tempest* could not have been played there.

2 Commentary

The aim of this commentary is to respond to the potential of the text without suggesting that any reading could be definitive. Throughout the commentary considerable attention is given to the range of possibilities available in a Renaissance staging, but the play has been, and will continue to be, produced in many different theatrical environments and my intention is not to suggest that a 'Renaissance' staging should be preferred to any other approach. The commentary on each scene begins with a consideration of key issues that contribute to our understanding of that scene, exploring its place in the structure of the play and any unusual elements that may determine our response to the whole scene, such as aspects of its staging. The aim of these sections is particularly to remind readers of factors that might be obvious to viewers but that emerge less readily in reading.

One key element that should be borne in mind throughout the commentary is that reading and seeing a play are very different experiences, no more so than in the question of how we receive information about who the characters are. In reading the play we are given information about the characters in different ways from when we see it. For example, in modern editions of *The Tempest* we are usually presented with texts where the names of the speakers are clearly identified for us by prefixes before each speech. This means that, for example, we know that Gonzalo, Antonio and Sebastian all speak in Act I, scene i, and we can probably check who they are against a cast list printed at the beginning of the play, which may give us not only their names but additional information about their family relationships or social status. In the theatre, however, we do not know who these characters are by name until Act II, scene i, and the task of working out what is going on is much more complex since the orderly succession of lines and stage directions in the printed text resolves itself into a range of different channels of communication. However, there may well be occasions when characters' physical appearance on stage may help us to identify them or clarify their relationships in ways that the text will not. In modern theatres we often have the help of a programme to identify the characters and their status but even if the characters are given in order of speaking it is not necessarily the easiest of tasks to work out in a darkened auditorium exactly who is speaking in the early stages of a production and what their relationships are.

The play is open to many potential readings and stagings but any one production must make choices from that range of options, choices which will in turn determine how other aspects of the play may be interpreted. Many of those choices are, or can be, determined by careful consideration of the script but there are also limits to what the script itself offers and also to what an audience can assimilate in a theatre without the opportunity to turn back the pages to scrutinize all the evidence relating to a particular point, or use the rewind facility on a recorded version to reconsider how a line was spoken.

Dramatis personae

The Folio includes a list of characters (dramatis personae) at the end of the text of *The Tempest* that helps to establish some of the key relationships for us, and most of that list of names pose few problems in terms of how we might imagine the characters. However, Ariel and Caliban pose some interesting questions that can colour a whole reading of the play, and both Miranda and Prospero exemplify some of the issues that are not covered by a cast list but will influence a staging of the play. It is generally assumed that in the Renaissance theatre, Ariel was probably played by the best singer amongst the young actors (often referred to as boys) who played female parts. Since the young actors routinely played women who dressed up as men, and since in this case Prospero tells Ariel to dress like a sea nymph and nymphs are traditionally female, it is hard to determine whether original audiences would have perceived Ariel as gendered in any significant way. In productions based on the 1667 Dryden/Davenant adaptation, which was the dominant theatrical version of *The Tempest* for many decades, and even once Shakespeare's play was regularly staged again after 1838, Ariel was usually played by a woman. Often this was a pragmatic response, both as a means of obtaining the services of a good singer who could achieve the ethereal quality demanded by Ariel's songs, which was usually felt to be best achieved by a female voice, and because the play had relatively few parts for the women who were otherwise employed as part of a theatre's resident company. As staffing practices changed and under the influence of the late nineteenth-century movement towards 'authentic' stagings (Styan), male Ariels became more common and the part is now regularly played by both male and female actors, usually without any suggestion of cross-gender casting: a male actor plays a male Ariel, a female actor a female Ariel. Ariel's gender can make a significant difference to the ways in which Prospero's treatment of Ariel is presented, particularly in terms of the master–servant relationship and the occasional hints of some kind of affection between them. As well as the many sea nymphs portrayed in paintings and literature, there is some guidance to suggest what a Renaissance Ariel might have looked like: as well as an extant costume design for a character called Ariel from one of Jonson's masques that suggests what an airy spirit might have looked like, there may be an even closer Renaissance source for Ariel's costume as sea nymph (Egan). Modern Ariels are very varied: from the boiler-suit clad Karl Johnson in Derek Jarman's film to the naked cherub of *Prospero's Books*, via the 'young and beautiful woman (Aunjanue Ellis)' in George C. Wolfe's 1995 New York staging (Coursen).

Most Ariels give the impression of being lithe and swift (though Simon Russell Beale in 1993 was a notable exception) but Caliban is generally seen as heavy and slow. The evidence from the play is that to most of the characters Caliban seems to be outside the bounds of what they construe to be normal but at the same time he has some human characteristics. In the Folio list of dramatis personae Caliban is referred to as a 'salvage and deformed slave'. In modern editions 'salvage' is usually modernized to 'savage', eliding the original

spelling with its connotations of woodlands, which caused Frank
Kermode to link the characterization of Caliban usefully with the
salvage men or wodwose familiar from such tales as *Sir Gawain and
The Green Knight* (Kermode). It may well be that we should not read
too much into this spelling but it would also be too dogmatic to
reject the idea that the European tradition of wild men of the woods
was part of the matrix that gave birth to the figure of Caliban. The
other characters' descriptions of Caliban appear to reveal as much
about the speaker as the person spoken about: Prospero's description
of him as 'a freckled whelp, hag-born' (I.ii.283) excited much
comment at the turn of the nineteenth century from commentators
who saw freckles as a characteristic peculiar to white people and
found a white savage hard to explain; Miranda thinks of him as a
man, Trinculo originally (on the basis of his outward appearance and
his smell) as a fish, but later, and more aptly, as not only one of the
original inhabitants of the island but also someone who could be
exhibited at a fair in England.

In a play much concerned with first impressions, with the difficulties of discerning true character beneath outward appearances,
and with the relativity of perception, it is not surprising that these
issues should arise in a close reading of the text, which will also,
for example, enable us to work out his age. On a stage, however,
Caliban must be embodied, given a physical presence based on
certain choices made about what the play suggests and how much
weight to put on certain issues. Those choices will, in turn, determine audiences' responses to what is presented to them, since they
will open up some possibilities and close others down. Caliban is
human enough to be able to use language, he can carry wood, he
can get drunk and he was able to attempt to rape Miranda. Equally
there is something about him that most of the people he meets
find monstrous: he is smelly, fish-like, he is called 'tortoise' and
'earth', a 'freckled whelp' and so on. He is in part a lineal descendant of the savage men who figure in older literature, so he could
simply be presented as no more than a wild man of the woods but
interpretations have varied widely (and wildly). He has been interpreted in various ways: as a wild man of the woods, an embodiment of a Darwinian missing link between the apes and

humankind, and in 1974 Peter Hall had him costumed as half beast, half noble savage, to stress his divided nature (see Chapter 4, 'Key Productions and Performances'). Theatrical choices have sometimes deliberately evoked black slavery: in some modern productions Caliban's monstrous 'otherness' has simply and powerfully been that he has been played by a black actor with no special make-up, in contrast to an otherwise white cast, so that his monstrosity is simply and strikingly being non-white, a powerful element in productions that stress the colonial element of the play. Thus, whatever decisions are made as to Caliban's physical appearance they can have a very powerful effect on how the play is understood by an audience.

In the case of Prospero, theatrical choices about his age can make a significant difference to how the play is interpreted by an audience. Prospero has often been seen as an old man because of the circumstances of his retiring from magic and the somewhat melancholy attitudes encapsulated in his statement that every third thought shall be his grave, but he need be no older than any father of a teenager, since a careful reading of the script indicates that Miranda is in her early teens. On that evidence Prospero could easily be in his early thirties or even younger, but other details suggest that he had ruled Milan for some time and so most Prosperos both in the theatre and in critical discourses are seen as considerably older. Indeed Prospero has often been seen as a literally patriarchal figure, particularly if the production or the critic has seen *The Tempest* as Shakespeare's farewell to his art and as some kind of valedictory theatrical retirement testament, all of which pushes the identification of Prospero with Shakespeare (and some Prosperos have even been made-up to resemble Shakespeare). But Shakespeare was not yet 50 when he wrote the play and although many European Renaissance men died earlier than many men do now, he was not an old man, nor in fact was *The Tempest* his last play. However, theatrically there could be a tension between Prospero as Miranda's father and Prospero as Mage-cum-duke-cum-Shakespeare-substitute, who has seemed to need to be presented as nearer whatever we may see as retirement age, which suggests someone who is in his 40s or older. Peter Greenaway's Prospero, Sir John Gielgud, was in his eighties when he last played the part but only 26 when he first played what was described as an unusually youthful Prospero in 1930. Clearly a theatrical interpretation will have to make some kind of choice about Prospero's physical appearance that will affect not only his relationship with Miranda but also how we see his time in Milan and his relationship with his, presumably younger, brother.

Miranda may seem relatively unproblematic as a character, since her main functions in the play are to be Prospero's audience when he tells her their story in Act I, scene ii, and then to fall in love with Ferdinand, but it is worth pointing out that, like Ariel, the part would originally have been written for and played by one of the trained youths who played the young romantic heroines in Renaissance plays. There do not appear to be any significant issues raised by this, other than the major one raised by the whole convention, which is the extent to which Renaissance audiences were routinely aware of the practice as an issue when watching plays, or whether it was foregrounded from time to time for some metatheatrical purpose.

ACT I

Act I, scene i

The first scene is short but characterized by the bustle of a nautical crisis, with much to-ing and fro-ing, whistles and, as the stage direction has it, confused noise. One important point that is often lost by readers is that in production, although the action clearly takes place on a ship, the audience does not know where it is, where it is going, where it has come from, what time of day it is or who is on board other than some sailors and some noblemen, unless the scene is staged so that they manage to hear above the din that there are a king and a prince on board. In production this tends to be obscured by the enthusiasm of those responsible for special effects unless, for example, the director chooses to freeze the storm noises so that the audience can hear the dialogue.

In a Renaissance staging the main stage area may have been the deck of the ship and the nobles might have appeared from below decks via a trap, while the upper level could have been used either for them or for the Master and Boatswain, with the invective being hurled from one level to another. Perhaps the Boatswain and the nobles were on the main stage with the Master above, shouting to each other. If both nobles and sailors used the main stage, stage doors could have been used to create a sense of confusion with characters jostling one another as they attempted to use the same entrances and exits. It is also tempting to think of ship's rigging being used in the scene in some ways, with ropes swinging and generally adding to the atmosphere of mayhem. The key point in all this is that there is no indication in the Folio of any attempt in the original production to stage a wreck in which an actual representation of a ship disappeared beneath any representation of waves. As the Romantic poet Samuel Taylor Coleridge argued, the storm scene is 'the bustle of a tempest, from which the real horrors are abstracted' (Hawkes).

Not very much later in the play we will discover that the supposed wreck was in fact a theatrical illusion, a spectacle created for the 'entertainment' of the passengers as well as for us. This ties in with the play's interest in the metatheatrical: clearly an audience always knows in some sense that the storm scene does not contain a real shipwreck, since it is an event within a staged fiction, but within the conventions that govern such stage wrecks it appears to be 'real'. In a play that turns out to be partly at least about the power of theatre, it is fitting that the opening should itself be an example of both Prospero's magic art and the art of the theatre. Many productions, particularly in the nineteenth-century theatre, went for full-blown representations of a practicable stage ship manoeuvring around an illusorily realistic ocean before sinking (see Chapter 4 for some examples). Often in such stagings the dialogue had to be cut since the stages were not big enough to accommodate full-sized ships with actual crews, and sometimes the effects were so spectacular that there was a long wait before the next scene could begin. Sometimes in production Ariel is present in the scene, the spirit's actions anticipating his description of them in Act I, scene ii, and sometimes in modern productions the action is preceded by some kind of enactment of elements of the back-story.

Although in performance the atmosphere of noisy confusion may hide the fact, the scene does introduce some important thematic elements which are ill served by a staging in which the dialogue is drowned out by the noise. The idea of a ship being in some ways a microcosm of the state is an ancient one and the scene raises the whole question of authority and its proper exercise in appropriate contexts, the relationship between order and disorder, nature and humankind, anarchy and government, self-control and social control and between the individual and society.

1–8   The play opens with the actual tempest. The first stage direction in the First Folio is 'A tempestuous noise of thunder and lightning heard' and it would make a greater impact if the noise started very suddenly at full power in an otherwise silent auditorium. Presumably the noise is backstage and probably also from above and below. The initial dialogue between the Master and Boatswain economically sets the scene with its urgent nautical terminology and the references to running aground, followed by the entrance of the mariners to act on the Boatswain's orders as they try to fight the storm. The exchanges are brief and the atmosphere is one of hurry, noise, whistles blowing, violence and disorder. Contemporary references indicate the extent to which the audience may have shared one or more contradictory views of sailors and their aptitudes. According to an officer writing to the Earl of Leicester in 1582, 'unruly mariners . . . may be as well void of reason as of obedience', or as Walter Ralegh put it, 'all discourse of magnanimity, of national virtue, of religion, of liberty, and whatsoever else hath wont to move and encourage virtuous men, hath no force at all with the common soldier [meaning sailor] in comparison of spoil and riches'. However, the Elizabethan admiral Sir William Monson had a higher opinion of the abilities of the boatswain: 'As the master commands the tacking of the ship, the hoisting or striking the yard, the taking in or putting forth the sails, upon the winding of the master's whistle the boatswain takes it with his, and sets the sailors with courage to do their work, every one of them knowing by their whistle what they are to do' (Rodger). In reading the scene, it appears as though Shakespeare was aware of these contradictory views and his original audiences may have been clearer about the details of the nautical manoeuvres than a modern audience would be. Apparently the mariners were using some innovative approaches to their particular problems, but how far the original audience would have been able to pick out these nuances is open to question since the key elements of the scene are confusion and disorder rather than clarity.

9–27   The arrival of the noblemen complicates both the stage picture and the scene, quickly establishing a conflict, with the courtiers trying to exert their usual authority but getting in the way of the seamen trying to save the ship. The contrast between the groups can be readily established if both groups are dressed in ways that emphasize their social status: the nobles in impractical fashion, probably their wedding finery if Gonzalo's comments in Act I, scene ii, are accurate; the sailors in suitable garb for rough weather. Both Alonso and Antonio ask for the Master, presumably as he is in charge, but the courtiers' attempts to exert their authority mar the labour of those who actually have authority in these special circumstances ('What cares these roarers for the name of king?', ll. 16–17).

28–33   The one character who has some opportunity to establish himself in the scene is Gonzalo, whose humorous speech alluding to the proverbial view that someone born to be hanged will never drown is not specifically addressed to anyone else (he may be briefly alone on stage) and can be played as an aside to the audience, both establishing a comic distance from the various storms and giving the audience a brief respite from the hurly-burly of the scene.

34–51   The dispute between the courtiers and the Boatswain is rekindled, with the Boatswain complaining bitterly about their futile interventions as he tries to go about his business. Sebastian and Antonio begin to be individualized through their characteristic tone of petulant carping while Gonzalo's wry contention that the Boatswain will not drown (ll. 46–8) again offers a kind of time out from the bustle of the storm. The stage direction 'Enter Mariners Wet' (presumably from a judicious backstage application of water) marks the end of the battle to save the ship.

52 to the end   If the staging allows them to be heard, Antonio and
Sebastian can further establish their quarrelsome natures with more
aspersions from the nobles on the Boatswain's character (ll. 54–7),
while Gonzalo continues his riff on the Boatswain's ultimate fate,
before another stage direction indicates 'a confused noise within',
with cries of 'Mercy on us! / We split, we split!, Farewell my wife and
children, Farewell brother' and 'We split, we split, we split' (ll. 60–2)
all suggesting the throes of the wreck. Out of the confused noise we
may be able to hear the references to wife, children and brother that
anticipate the play's stress on splitting and reuniting families, before
the scene resolves itself into more choric lines from Gonzalo.

Act I, scene ii

The scene that follows is in marked contrast to the storm, but it is
easy for a reader, following the orderly succession of lines on a page,
to underestimate the series of shocks and dislocations that the play
offers in performance. First, the play starts with a literal bang, the
'tempestuous noise of thunder and lightning', where one might have
expected a low-key dialogue or a prologue speech. That scene is
clearly set on a ship; it is loud, noisy and, as it turns out, short. The
next scene is clearly not on the ship, it is much quieter and it involves
a completely different group of characters. Initially we have no idea
what the relationships between the first scene and the second scene
are, though the conventions and dynamics of drama suggest that
there will be some relationship between them. The change from the
wreck scene to the appearance of Prospero and Miranda can be
crucial in establishing the tone of the production. If Prospero and
Miranda immediately come into the same space that has just been
occupied by the storm scene, there will be very different resonances
than if they are in a clearly different space or, as sometimes happens
in the theatre, there is some kind of pause to remove the setting from
the first scene. It is possible for a fluid staging to give an audience a
sense that the new characters are occupying not only the same stage
space but also the same imagined space as the previous ones, thus
beginning to dispel any sense of the reality of the storm scene, a
process which is then furthered by the dialogue between Prospero

and Miranda. So, whereas the first scene may have been a spectacular thematic exposition, this one has to convey the context for the wreck, explain who the characters are, and the relevant parts of their histories, and establish the play's ground rules, particularly as they will involve not just a normal amount of suspending disbelief but also the necessity for us to accept Prospero's magic powers and the existence of supernatural creatures.

As in the first scene, it is important that, at this stage, we have no idea who is speaking or, initially, where we are. Some 500 lines long (nearly a quarter of the play), this scene involves Prospero and Miranda on stage throughout (although she is asleep for some 120 lines) as they are joined by a succession of individuals (Ariel, Caliban and Ferdinand), so that the basic mode of the scene is calmer and more static than Act I, scene i, with two people being joined in turn by a single character, who leaves before the next one appears, until the end of the scene when Ariel is present at the same time as Ferdinand from line 373. The dialogue is more orderly, with only two characters speaking to each other, until Caliban's appearance at line 321 when Prospero, Caliban and Miranda each speak, although editors have often taken Miranda's speech (ll. 350–61) away from her and given it to Prospero as part of a process of making her behaviour more appropriate to what they considered to be the norms for a virginal adolescent. The stage space is not cluttered with other people, there is no rushing to and fro and there are no stage directions for storm noises so the space assumes a quite different atmosphere from that of Act I, scene i.

Miranda's opening speech (ll. 1–13) not only establishes a family relationship (father/daughter) with the other person on stage but calls into question what we think we have just seen, by challenging the apparent nature of the storm, which, we now realize, may not have been natural after all. This scene needs to create some of the key tensions in the play, and does so out of the conflicting needs of the two characters: Miranda wants Prospero to end the storm, Prospero needs to tell Miranda what is going on, to prepare her for the events of the day. One of the significant characteristics of this play is that there is a major tension between the type of story that is to be told and the means adopted to tell it. In *The Tempest*, Shakespeare was experimenting with a structure that enabled him to tackle a romance theme within a more neo-classical structure than was usual for him. Of course, his early play *The Comedy of Errors* depended partly on the Aristotelian tension created by the framing device of the imminent execution of the father, but in *The Tempest* there is an emphasis on the neo-classical unities that is surprising in a dramatist whose career-long penchant had been for a much more epic style (see Chapter 3, 'The Play's Sources and Cultural Context'). In *The Tempest*, however, Shakespeare sets the play in a single place, the island (neo-classical critics were divided as to whether the sea could be counted as part of a single location); insists, on several occasions, that the time of the action is identical to the time of the representation; and, at least arguably, presents a single action, in which Prospero finds a way to recover his dukedom in the face of a range of obstacles. This puts a particular strain on the exposition since this approach means that Shakespeare is faced with narrating rather than dramatizing events which elsewhere might have formed the first two or three Acts of his play. In *The Winter's Tale*, for example, the events dealing with the grown-up child are staged only in the second part of the play (Acts IV and V), while the circumstances of how she came to be in her place of exile are staged in great detail for the first three Acts, in which she figures solely as the pregnant Hermione's property bump. Choosing to stage what is in effect the narrative's second shipwreck (Prospero and Miranda's arrival on the island being the first) as the first scene of the play, puts even greater pressure on the second scene, since the focus switches immediately from a large group of mainly unidentifiable characters that we have only just been introduced to (some of whom will not reappear until near the end of Act V) to another group who are very gradually introduced throughout Act I, scene ii.

Prospero is initially wearing clothes (his 'magic garment', line 24) that embody in some ways his magician status, and he will later present himself in clothes appropriate to the Duke of Milan, but when he takes his magic robe off at line 24 there is no indication of what he is wearing as his everyday clothes. Nevertheless, his changes of clothing are important in suggesting his changing roles within the play. There are no indications of what Miranda is wearing at any point in the action. Although Ferdinand will later assume that she is a goddess, there is no suggestion that this stems from her clothing rather than from the situation and perhaps her beauty. Nor are we encouraged to speculate that when Gonzalo was equipping the boat twelve years previously he foresaw the clothing needs of an adolescent girl or that Ariel had a special gift for tailoring – *The Tempest* is not that kind of narrative and it does not operate by the kind of conventions that demand an explanation for every detail of everyday life on the island.

1–186 The first section of dialogue establishes both the father–daughter relationship between Prospero and Miranda and the story of how they came to be on the island and it also establishes that what we have just seen is not quite what we thought we saw. The apparent reality of the first scene is revealed both as part of Prospero's magic and as an example of the magic of the theatre. The discrepancy between seeing and believing/hearing is established here (and the more realistic the staging of the storm scene, the greater the discrepancy between the evidence of ears and eyes) and is a significant part of the play's structure of testing modes of perception and modes of experience against one another.

The actors are faced with significant challenges in Prospero's lengthy exposition of the circumstances that brought him and Miranda to the island, since the amount of information to be conveyed demands skilled acting to vary the pace vocally and through gesture. Prospero's narrative lasts some 120 lines, punctuated by concern that his story isn't getting through to his daughter (and, by extension, his audience) and by occasional brief interventions from Miranda. He tells her to sit, at line 32, and says that he will 'arise', at line 168, but there are no Folio stage directions until Ariel's entrance at line 188. Orgel assumes that both Prospero and Miranda sit at line 32 but the actor playing Prospero is unlikely to want to sit throughout the whole sequence. The interaction between father and daughter throughout this scene is crucial to creating the play's dynamic: Prospero's speeches are long and unless he varies his position by jumping up or pacing about while telling Miranda her history the action is relatively static. Miranda's role becomes entirely reactive and she never speaks more than three and a half lines at one time, so she too has much to convey mainly wordlessly as she listens to Prospero's narrative.

1–24 Presumably Miranda and Prospero enter separately rather than coming on together and the relationship between them can be conveyed visually by their stances: she may well move distractedly, while he is more stationary until line 13. Miranda's first speech swiftly establishes a change of tone, rhythm and focus, compared with the first scene. The switch from prose to verse and the length of the speech in themselves impose an order absent from the earlier scene. Her first words also unsettle our assumptions about that scene by suggesting that the storm was staged by Prospero's 'art' and that he has powers to calm the wild waters (ll. 1–2).The lines economically establish the father–daughter relationship and Prospero's magician status as well as Miranda's role as someone who has watched events from a different viewpoint from the audience's: whereas we were watching and hearing crew and passengers who believed they were being shipwrecked, Miranda had a more distant view, concentrating on the 'brave vessel' (l. 6). Already the character and the audience have different perspectives on the first scene, and Prospero then challenges Miranda's implied criticism in 'Had I been any god of power' (ll. 10–13) with three brief imperative statements (ll. 13–15), that suggest a slowing down of the rhythm through the largely monosyllabic brevity of each statement, and the division of Prospero's second line by splitting it between the two characters. The gaps between statements could be read as implying that Prospero is offering Miranda some kind of paternal embrace to soothe her, although he is not given any stage direction to that effect in the tripartite breakdown. There is a good opportunity here to establish the nature of their relationship through grouping and gesture, and a Prospero who stands apart from Miranda will seem very different from one who doesn't. Prospero's repetition of 'no harm', and then 'thee' in 'thee, my dear one, thee, my daughter' (ll. 15–17) might both suggest a parent soothing a child by repetition and also act as a reminder to the audience of the importance of this key family relationship. When Prospero names himself (l. 20) he begins a process of naming that will eventually allow us to plot the various other important family relationships in the play. When he removes his 'magic garment' (l. 24) he is also moving from action to family history, while associating his control over nature with the paraphernalia of magic.

25–33   Very early in this sequence Prospero forces us into one of the play's characteristic reversals of point of view when he tells Miranda that it was not a wreck but a 'direful spectacle' (l. 26) of a wreck that she just saw and that, even though we may have shared Miranda's perception that the creatures all perished, no one was hurt. Prospero underlines the point for his audiences on stage and in the auditorium with his repeated use of 'which' in:

> there is no soul,
> No, not so much perdition as an hair
> Betid to any creature in the vessel
> Which thou heard'st cry, which thou saw'st sink   (ll. 29–32)

In the first scene we had assumed that the usual theatrical convention was operating: we were watching fictions that we agree for the purposes of the drama to be real; but that understanding is now undercut by Prospero's revelation that the wreck, which we took to be a 'real' event within the fictional world, was not in fact real but instead an orchestrated performance.

34–52   Prospero's urgency comes across in the imperatives in line 38 ('Obey, and be attentive') as he tries to find a suitable starting point for his story with his question about the earliest things Miranda can remember. An actor playing Prospero might find a clue in 'person' (l. 42) to call to his mind an image of Miranda's mother to underpin the next few lines, only to be thrown off course by her remembering, questioningly, the women who attended her (l. 47). Prospero, incidentally offering a clue to her age (l. 41), then names her for the first time (l. 48), before she cuts off their peering into 'the dark backward and abyss of time' with the deflating monosyllables of 'But that I do not' (l. 52).

53–116   There are opportunities to vary the tone here, with Miranda's misunderstanding the import of Prospero's 'Thy father was the Duke of Milan' (l. 54) leading to Prospero's slightly forced but comic misogynistic reference to her mother (ll. 56–7). Prospero's confirmation that he is indeed Miranda's father (ll. 56–9) is couched in his characteristically tortuous syntax, which editors often try to emend, although actors can use it as a way into his character. Prospero often seems distracted in this scene, as though the effort of remembering scrambles his ability to formulate his thoughts. His response after Miranda's eager question about whether it was a good or bad thing that they left Milan (ll. 60–1) can readily be approached as an effort to refocus his brain, with the repetition of 'both' suggesting him coming back to the present and then picking up her thought in his 'as thou sayst' (ll. 61–2). Miranda is then apparently left hanging in the middle of a line at the caesura, before encouraging him with 'Please you, farther', which an audience will probably hear as 'father' as well as 'go on'. There seem to be a number of opportunities here for both movement and gesture, depending on the actors' interpretation of their roles. Prospero follows the oral pun on 'father' with his first mention of Antonio, again in a tortuous syntax with a concatenation of unexpected word orders that suggests his mental strain. Moreover, 'farther' gives way to 'My brother . . . thy uncle . . . Antonio . . . I . . . thee . . . me . . . brother . . . he . . . thyself', a total of 11 out of 23 words in three lines (ll. 66–8) attempting to hold family relationships in some sort of grammatical relationship. The rush of words is punctuated by a sudden worry that he has lost his audience:

> Dost thou attend me?
> MIRANDA   Sir, most heedfully.   (l. 78)

but it scarcely interrupts the flow of his speech denouncing his brother, until another sudden moment of doubt,

> thou attend'st not!
> MIRANDA   O, good sir, I do!
> PROSPERO   I pray thee mark me.   (ll. 87–8)

Prospero navigates his way through another brief exchange with Miranda that scarcely interrupts his grammatical flow ('Dost thou

hear? / MIRANDA   Your tale, sir, would cure deafness', l. 106), piling
up an incidental theatrical metaphor (l. 107) and the first reference to
the King of Naples before finally letting Miranda back into the discussion at line 116.

116–86   Miranda's brief interruptions have thus far mainly served
to vary the pace, allow the actor playing Prospero opportunities to
conserve his breath, and guard against the audience losing concen-
tration, but this one allows her to pick up the misogynist tone of
Prospero's mention of her mother's chastity with a similar, perhaps
rather prim, remark about her grandmother (ll. 118–20). Once again
this scarcely seems to register with Prospero as he continues his
story, although lines 135–8 offer the promise to both Miranda and the
audience that their close attention to his story will repay them. At
line 161 Prospero adds another name to the grid, introducing
Gonzalo's crucial role and supplying the circumstantial evidence of
how he was able to organize his life and continue his studies.
Miranda's enthusiastic wish to see Gonzalo (ll. 168–9) may be shared
by the audience but Prospero fails to respond. Dramatic logic
appears to be leading us towards such an appearance and Prospero,
getting up ('Now I arise', l. 169), while telling Miranda to stay sitting,
appears to mark the end of the exposition as he prepares for more
action. Somewhere between line 169 and line 187 ('I am ready now')
he presumably puts on his magic garment again. By now Miranda
completely accepts that he is responsible for the storm (ll. 177–8).
Perhaps the fact that Prospero has to send Miranda to sleep at line 186
in order to continue with his plot is indicative of the difficulties that
Shakespeare had in organizing the dynamics of the narrative. Some
commentators have accused Shakespeare of sending audiences to
sleep as well as Miranda and have worried at his power to control the
action as absolutely as he does in lines 184–6.

187–8   Prospero's first call to Ariel can be played simply to suggest
that it takes a few moments for Ariel to hear him, or if, as Orgel
suggests, he puts his cloak on during line 187, as though Ariel
responds to the magic properties symbolized by the cloak. It can
even be used to suggest some of the antagonisms between the two,

depending on when Ariel actually appears and the tone of voice
Prospero uses. At this stage Shakespeare offers no verbal clues as to
what Ariel may have looked like, but given that the spirit is later
dressed as a sea nymph and that he has to sing and perform music,
the role was presumably originally played by an accomplished young
player with a good singing voice who usually played female roles.

189–93   Ariel's opening lines swiftly change the tone of the scene as
he establishes his supernatural status through claims to be at home in
three of the four elements (air, water and fire, but significantly, not
earth) and through the change in diction from Prospero's complex
grammar and vocabulary as Ariel tends towards the monosyllabic,
simpler syntax and listing as his initial mode of communication.

194–210   Prospero's relationship with Ariel differs significantly
from what we have just seen between him and Miranda. He is now in
the position of asking the questions while Ariel supplies further
insights into the first scene, which have sometimes been taken as
retrospective stage directions and interpreted fairly literally, particularly by those who favour a realistic shipwreck. Clearly Ariel's
account of the shipwreck (ll. 196–237), with a description of St Elmo's
Fire (ll. 196–201) that is probably indebted to Strachey's account of
the wreck of the *Sea Venture* (see Chapter 3, 'The Play's Sources and
Cultural Context'), supplements what Shakespeare has presented in
Act I, scene i. But, in the theatre, whether it is an accurate version of
that scene or not will depend on the decisions taken about how to
stage the first scene. Ariel's narrative can be made literally accurate by
staging that first scene in a way that reflects his story; it can be seen
as supplementing the staging; or it can be presented as at variance
with that staging, so that the possibilities for disorientating the audience here are high.

211–37   In this sequence, Ariel also introduces us to the king's son
Ferdinand by name (l. 212), and ties up the fates of the various denizens
of the ship, although he does not specifically mention Trinculo and
Stephano. He assures us that the nobles have been landed on the
island with their garments still unspoiled by the apparent wreck and

he again stresses the illusory nature of that event when he talks about the rest of the fleet supposing that they saw the ship sink (ll. 232–7), further developing one of the recurring themes of the play, the discrepancy between appearances and reality, between what actually happened and what we thought happened.

237–300   The old view of Prospero as an untroubled, even serene mage does not sit easily with the rather tetchy relationship with Ariel revealed in these lines. It is just after two o'clock when Prospero and Ariel first discuss the time and Prospero insists that they will need to get everything sorted by six (ll. 239–41). This is very roughly the timetable for the performance of a play at the Globe, another example of the metatheatrical tendencies of *The Tempest*, which keeps on drawing attention to its status as a play and to the discrepancies between events and the perception of those events. Ariel's relationship with Prospero comes into sharper focus as his delight in creating the wreck gives way to complaints about his servitude. Ariel is a bondsman with a date of release from service: like many of the early settlers of the new world he is indentured, bound to serve for a period of years, which in his case is on the point of expiry. Although the exchanges between Prospero and Ariel flesh out much of the play's prehistory, much of the information is not strictly relevant to the development of the plot, even if it explains some of the reasons why both Ariel and Caliban (who we are yet to meet) are not entirely happy with their relationship with Prospero. At a realistic level, it also involves Prospero reminding Ariel of facts and events that he can only know because Ariel told him about them in the first place, thus encapsulating one of the perennial problems of dramatic exposition and also manifesting some of the problems that can arise when a dramatist attempts to bring epic material into theatrical focus. One important function of this discussion between Ariel and Prospero is that it helps to further our sense of this dramatic world as one where the usual order of existence is somehow suspended and distanced in favour of one where the boundaries between the human and the non-human, the animate and the inanimate are changed from the normal, as a strange and magic atmosphere is created by all the references to unnatural phenomena such as doing business 'in the veins

o'th' earth' (l. 255) or being confined in pine trees or oaks. Ariel's
vocabulary shows him as anxious to present himself as a spirit of the
air, fire and water, as opposed to Caliban, who is associated with the
earth.

301–4   At the end of Prospero and Ariel's dialogue Prospero
instructs Ariel to be invisible, and to make himself like a nymph of
the sea. Unless one assumes that being dressed like a sea nymph is
meant to be a conventional marker of invisibility, as some scholars
have, the two commands appear to be contradictory and it is point-
less for Ariel to look like a sea nymph if no one on stage is going to
see him except Prospero. Equally there is no obvious reason why
Ariel should not have been costumed as a sea nymph from when he
first appeared (Ariels who appear in 1.1 are sometimes so dressed for
the purposes of 'sinking' the ship, although they may also be dressed
as spirits of the air, particularly if they are made to fly in that scene).
In performance, however, the audience will see Ariel and we will be
offered many of the pleasures of dramatic irony as a result of our
being in the know about something that will be concealed from all
the other characters in the play.

305–18   When Ariel has gone off to make himself like a sea nymph,
the subsequent sequence (ll. 307–18) appears to be designed mainly to
create a series of important visual contrasts. Prospero wakes Miranda
and proposes that they should go to see Caliban, of whom we have
already heard something in Prospero and Ariel's exchanges. Miranda,
who is, of course, unaware of what has gone on while she was asleep,
confirms our sense of Caliban's otherness (ll. 309–10) and Prospero
enhances it with his use of terms like 'slave', 'earth', and 'tortoise',
which contrast with Ariel, the servant associated with air, fire and
water. Caliban is clearly a deliberate foil for Ariel: the main difference
between them is that Caliban appears to be simply a slave with no
agreed date of manumission. Ariel performs magic, Caliban brings in
wood, but both Ariel and Caliban resent their servitude to Prospero.

However, Shakespeare chooses to create a series of visual
contrasts (which may be strengthened if Prospero wears the magic
garment he took off earlier in the scene whenever he is performing

magic). The sequence may involve Prospero dressed conventionally as a magician, addressing a being who may have been dressed as an airy spirit (as the dramatis personae suggests), before waking his daughter (possibly wearing clothes that will legitimize Ferdinand mistaking her for a goddess) and then suggesting that they visit his slave Caliban. Prospero then refers to Caliban as 'earth' (l. 314), having previously described him as a 'freckled whelp, hag-born – not honoured with / A human shape' (l. 283), and, after Caliban replies from off stage, as a 'tortoise', presumably referring to his dilatoriness but also suggesting a reptilian figure. Whatever precise decisions have been made about Caliban's appearance, the audience has been conditioned to expect something spectacularly abhorrent and aberrant. However, immediately after Prospero's remark, instead of the expected appearance of this monstrous figure, we see Ariel dressed as a sea nymph, once more confounding our expectation. Shakespeare is engineering an emblematic moment here utilizing defeated expectation and discrepant levels of awareness, as we see Ariel (but Miranda doesn't) when we have been led to expect a first sight of the monstrous Caliban.

319–30 Caliban talks about being styed in a hard rock (ll. 342–3) and Miranda says he has been 'Deservedly confined into this rock' (l. 360), so, given the stress on his earthiness, it would have been logical for him to have crawled, tortoise-like, either from the discovery space at the back of a Renaissance stage or from the trapdoor. Wherever he makes his entrance from, Caliban's initial appearance will settle some of the doubts the audience may have had about him. Prospero has stressed his earthy reptilian qualities; Miranda apparently sees him as human, since she later describes Ferdinand as the third man she has ever seen (Prospero is the first and Caliban is the only other candidate for the second); later, Trinculo initially thinks Caliban is a fish but then settles for a dead native of the island. Terms like 'mooncalf' and 'monster' that are applied to him subsequent to this appearance clearly indicate that Caliban is not 'normal', but the exact nature of his abnormality depends on a range of theatrical choices.

The play's first scene is largely in prose, the second is in

Shakespeare's usual blank verse, except for Ariel's songs, and it is important that when Caliban appears (l. 321) he speaks in the same mode as the other characters (although he will speak prose with Trinculo and Stephano later) and matches Prospero's vehemence ('poisonous slave', 'wicked dam', ll. 320–1) with some colourful curses of his own:

> As wicked dew as e'er my mother brushed
> With raven's feather from unwholesome fen
> Drop on you both! A south-west blow on ye
> And blister you all o'er!   (ll. 321–4)

As this demonstrates, Caliban is not a simple lower-class character with access only to the prosaic register of speech. In this scene of contrasts he sees himself as a potential suitor to Miranda, anticipating the imminent arrival of her proper suitor, Ferdinand. If Ariel is played by a woman, when the character is sometimes seen as virtually another daughter or a faint echo of a love interest for Prospero, the range of contrasts established in this scene is further enhanced with different versions of 'beauty' and a 'beast', age and youth, 'normal' and 'monstrous', male and female (possibly with a male actor playing Ariel dressed as a female sea nymph), reflecting and refracting each other in a prismatic way.

331–73   Unlike Ariel, Caliban contests Prospero's account of his history, making the point that Prospero too is a usurper, and anticipating the ways he will behave when he encounters Trinculo and Stephano later. Miranda's speech beginning 'Abhorred slave' (ll. 350–61) has sometimes been given by editors and directors to Prospero (see Chapter 1, 'The Text and Early Performances') but it is consistent with some of her other statements and there seems no reason why it should be taken from her. After all, it was her that Caliban attempted to rape. The prismatic contrasts of the sequence that began with the introduction of the first supernatural character at line 189 culminate with the arrival of Ariel and Ferdinand, at line 373, which opens up the possibility of useful visual juxtapositions for the audience. The stage picture can be engineered to enable a brief moment of visual contrast between Caliban and Ariel or Caliban and Ferdinand or possibly Caliban and both Ariel and Ferdinand.

374–408 The invisible Ariel's song is in marked contrast to anything heard so far and it once again reframes the action. The dramaturgy is particularly skilful here, since the audience is not expecting Ferdinand and he probably has not been seen previously at all, unless a director chooses to follow the Folio stage direction by having him appear in Act I, scene i, and we have no idea how he fits into Prospero's plans. Ferdinand is unable to identify whether the source of the music is in the air or in the earth and then hears it above him, which suggest that Ariel's companions could have been located either in the music room above the stage or even under the stage (as in the case of the oboes in *Antony and Cleopatra*), any of which would help to increase the audience's sense of something unnatural since there would be no visible source of the music except for Ariel. At a time when music could only be played live, the absence of an obvious source for that music would have a greater impact than it might in an age of digital reproduction and broadcasting of sound. Interestingly, editors tend to assume that the term 'dispersedly' (l. 381) applied to the refrain means 'not in unison', as opposed to the view of directors, who often interpret it to mean scattered around the stage area, a reading supported by the *Oxford English Dictionary*'s entry for 'dispersedly'.

The invitation to Ferdinand to come to the yellow sands is followed by the haunting evocation of Ferdinand's dead father Alonso with the image of his bones becoming coral and everything suffering a 'sea-change' (ll. 398–405). Even the syntax here underscores the atmosphere of dislocation:

> Sitting on a bank,
> Weeping again the King my father's wreck,
> This music crept by me upon the waters

says Ferdinand, and the dislocation of the grammar conveys a powerful sense of his own passive and withdrawn state of mind.

409 to the end   Prospero draws Miranda's attention to Ferdinand only after some thirty lines of Ariel's songs and Ferdinand's soliloquy. At this point Ferdinand still believes that the rest of the passengers and crew have perished, so Ariel and Miranda and Prospero's onstage presence is important in defusing the tragic overtones of Ferdinand's belief in his father's death by contextualizing it as a situation contrived by Prospero. Prospero and Ariel's onstage presence also helps to distance the wooing scene, reducing some of its inherent improbability as Ferdinand moves virtually seamlessly from grief for his father to his amorous encounter with Miranda. When Ferdinand first sees Miranda he greets her with 'Most sure, the goddess / On whom these airs attend' (ll. 422–3), echoing a speech from the *Aeneid* in which Aeneas does actually speak to a goddess (see Chapter 3, 'The Play's Sources and Cultural Context', for the relationship between *The Tempest* and the *Aeneid*), but he then moves within seven lines from thinking she is a goddess to asking if she is a maid, encompassing the senses of 'human' and 'unmarried'. As Prospero remarks 'At the first sight / They have changed eyes' (ll. 441–2). Once Ferdinand and Miranda meet there is no conventional romantic plot in *The Tempest*. Whereas in traditional romantic comedies like *A Midsummer Night's Dream* or *As You Like It* there are a number of possible candidates for romantic partners, in Shakespeare's late plays there is seldom any doubt about the outcome of a relationship: Miranda, and Perdita in *The Winter's Tale*, have no other suitors and in Miranda's case there is no dramatic tension in her relationship with Ferdinand other than what Prospero provides. Ferdinand's third speech to Miranda is his promise to make her Queen of Naples, and in making this promise, he appears to be ignoring Prospero's attempts to intervene. The romantic comedy dynamic depends not on other potential suitors or on lovers' tiffs but on Prospero being presented as a traditional comic father figure, suspicious of his offspring's sexuality and concerned about pre-marital sex. His worries do, of course, relate to the dynastic politics underlying his desire to bring Ferdinand and Miranda together, but it also seems that he invents obstacles ('this swift business / I must uneasy make lest too light winning / Make the prize light', ll. 452–3). In the flow of performance when we have no idea, at first sight, what may be about to happen next and have no opportunity to revisit Prospero's remarks, it is unlikely that an audience will wonder too much about an element that, as Stephen Orgel drily remarks, has 'generally been found unconvincing' by critics (Orgel, note to I.ii.452–3).

Prospero is playing psychological games with Ferdinand here since he knows that Alonso is still alive, so while his challenge to Ferdinand has some basis in truth there is no way that Ferdinand can be aware that it is true. It is noteworthy that Prospero chooses to regard Ferdinand as a would-be usurper (l. 454), thus locating him, in dynastic terms, as the true son of Alonso, but also demonstrating his own preoccupations and preconceptions, perhaps through a form of psychological leakage in which the game becomes something more like a restaging of his difficulties with Ferdinand's father and his own brother: one of the first things he says to Ferdinand is the accusation that Ferdinand is premature in assuming himself to be ruler of Naples, and subsequently that he is trying to gain control of the island from Prospero. From Prospero's asides we can gain a sense of the extent to which this whole scene of conflict between him and Ferdinand is manufactured, and that he is to some extent deliberately playing the role of the suspicious ruler and father, but clearly Miranda is unaware of the extent of the role-playing.

When Ferdinand attempts to resist Prospero's threats the stage direction says that 'He draws and is charmed from moving' (l. 467). Since Ariel is still on stage this looks like a good opportunity for him to be involved in the action.

Once Ferdinand and Miranda have met, and the dynastic solution to Prospero's problem of regaining Milan has been established, in the absence of any other serious suitors Prospero chooses to invent obstacles to the course of true love. Interestingly, Dryden and Davenant in their very successful adaptation of the play (see Chapter 4) chose to address this issue by introducing a standard romantic cross-purposes plot by giving Miranda a sister Dorinda and adding a second male suitor Hippolito (meant to be played by a woman). In Shakespeare's play, from Prospero's point of view, dealing with the future is relatively straightforward but, while the next generation may have been sorted out, there is still the *Realpolitik* of the present situation to deal with: as well as Alonso and Ferdinand, both Antonio and Sebastian need to be neutralized. Perhaps the reason that Shakespeare chose to deal with the supposed threat from Ferdinand as a usurper at this stage is that it is probably easier for an audience to accept Ferdinand uncritically as a romantic hero if they have not yet been introduced to his father and have not yet seen the serious plotting that will come in Act II, scene i.

ACT II

Act II, scene i

The clearing of a group of characters on a Renaissance stage often suggested a change of location. When Prospero, Ariel, Ferdinand and Miranda go off at the end of Act I, the nobles come on. They might have been physically very close, offering a brief moment of near physical juxtaposition and therefore a potential resolution of Ferdinand's and Alonso's dilemmas that would offer an interesting visual anticipation of the future outcome of the narrative.

Following Act I, scene ii, this is another long scene (325 lines) but here the dramatis personae are fixed until Ariel intervenes to thwart the renewed conspiracy. Alonso is both the main focus of attention and a virtually silent participant in the scene for its first third. The reactions of Gonzalo and Francisco suggest great concern for the king but he is clearly isolated verbally and probably physically. Similarly Antonio and Sebastian appear to be a pair and physically distant from Alonso and Gonzalo throughout the scene, since much of their dialogue is addressed to each other even if at times it seems designed to be overheard by its targets. Shakespeare uses dramatic irony throughout this scene since one of the key factors for Alonso and for Sebastian and Antonio is their assumption that Ferdinand had died in the wreck. We, of course, have just seen him and are aware that his concern for his supposedly dead father has been replaced by his desire for Miranda. In the theatre this scene needs careful handling to create an appropriate momentum to maintain audience interest, because of its length, its relatively slow pace, the need to establish the characters of the four main protagonists Alonso, Gonzalo, Antonio and Sebastian, and the fact that some of the characters have to go to sleep, which can raise the issue of over-contrivance again. As in the play's opening scene, it is important that we do not know initially who the characters on stage in this scene actually are, even if we do as we read. Clearly we have a fair idea that these characters are in some way related to those that Prospero spoke of in the second scene but the exact identifications take some time, and perhaps this helps us to navigate our way through the scene as we search for clarifications.

1–10 Gonzalo's focus on Alonso and his use of 'sir' (I.i) points to Alonso's status, and his proverbial discourse helps to identify him as the counsellor from Act I, scene i. This brief sequence establishes the pattern of the scene, in which Gonzalo attempts to cheer the king up while Alonso responds tersely.

11–70 Much of what goes on in the early part of this sequence is deliberately inconsequential, as Gonzalo tries to distract Alonso from his terrible personal and political situation while being constantly undercut by carping asides from Antonio and Sebastian. Alonso is clearly in no mood to be distracted from his grief as his very brief comments indicate: 'Prithee peace' (l. 9) stops Gonzalo long enough for Sebastian and Antonio's first comments on Gonzalo, while 'I prithee spare' (l. 26) allows Adrian to take up the conversational baton from Gonzalo. Adrian is in fact the first person identified by name (l. 29), although Prospero did not mention him earlier and he will turn out to be a minor character who, with Francisco, mainly serves to give us a sense of the size of the court. His main contribution is to introduce the thematically important discussion of the nature of the landscape and the state of their clothing (ll. 36–70). The nobles have very different perspectives on these topics with Adrian and Gonzalo in the optimistic camp while Sebastian and Antonio see only a hostile landscape and ruined clothes. The audience can assume legitimately that the different noblemen see things differently because of their own characters, not because of any reality visible to the audience. With the clothes we have Ariel's word that the nobles arrived with their garments unblemished and we presumably have our own eyes' evidence that this is the case. Although the mariners did make one of their entrances 'wet', we know that the theatre companies often spent very large sums on costume so not only is it dramatically unlikely that we are expected to see the noblemen's clothes as spoiled but it is also economically and theatrically unlikely that this was the case. Nevertheless, this scene partakes of one of the play's characteristic modes of development as we hear and see different versions of the evidence being presented to us, so that we are forced into an active role in making decisions about what version of events or which character is most trustworthy. This is one of those occasions when Renaissance dramaturgy had the advantage over the more realistic modes of staging that have been prevalent since that period: in a 'realistic' staging the production has to come down on one side or the other in the debate about the island's appearance and the nobles' clothing.

The discussion about clothing leads to more exposition, this time of the reasons for the voyage that led to the wreck, since Gonzalo tells us why the Neapolitans' ship was in a position to be wrecked close to Prospero's island, with the news of Alonso's daughter's marriage in Africa (ll. 68–70). The name Claribel adds another person to our chart of the family but, like Adrian, she will turn out to be something of a false start since she will never appear. For the literal-minded who have worried away at Ariel's reference to the Bermudas, this exposition should scotch any doubts that the imaginary island is meant to be in the Mediterranean, since not only did the 'rotten butt' that Prospero and Miranda sailed in arrive there, having left Italy, but so did the Neapolitans and Milanese who were journeying between Naples and Tunis. Indeed, although when Antonio and Sebastian are plotting they make the hyperbolic point that the distances involved in travel between Italy and Tunis are so long that it will take years to travel them, they are themselves on the return leg of a journey to Tunis. This is not to deny the vast importance the American voyages have for the play's setting and atmosphere, but it is worth reminding oneself that Ariel's trip to the 'still-vexed' Bermudas was itself a long-haul flight, not a short hop from the Mediterranean.

71–103 It is very difficult to convey the detailed nuances of the discussion about Tunis, Carthage and Dido in the theatre. The argument draws both on Virgil's *Aeneid* and on other interpretations of Dido that are likely to be very unfamiliar to a modern audience (see Orgel, pp. 39–43, and Hulme and Sherman) and probably the most that many members of a modern audience will get from this sequence is the fact that the characters clash over their interpretations.

104–40 Alonso is finally established as the ruler of Milan and Naples and Ferdinand's father, when he says

> O thou mine heir
> Of Naples and Milan, what strange fish
> Hath made his meal on thee?   (ll. 109–10)

The vehemence of his expressions of despair is undercut by the audience's awareness that Ferdinand is not only alive but in love. Francisco, a very minor attendant lord with only one other line in the play, then offers a spirited counterview (ll. 111–20) to Alonso's conclusion that he has failed as both ruler and father. While Francisco's words actually match what we have seen to be the reality of Ferdinand's fate, his poetic rhetoric can scarcely counter Alonso's flat, monosyllabic 'No, no he's gone' (l. 120). Sebastian, however, is keen to point out Alonso's failures and it is important for the actor to try to convey some of the underlying politics here. In dynastic terms, if the nobles can get back to Italy Sebastian will turn out to be the main beneficiary of the supposed loss of Ferdinand and the absence of Claribel and her husband. Alonso believes that he has played a diplomatic card by marrying his daughter to a foreign prince, one no doubt important for reasons of trade and political power, but in so doing he has lost his major dynastic asset, his son and heir. Some of the original audience may have been familiar with aspects of the politics of the Mediterranean and the role of English and other pirates who operated out of ports like Tunis, and the unease about the marriage apparently expressed by Alonso's courtiers and Claribel (ll. 126–9) may have conveyed an undercurrent of anti-Muslim sentiment to them.

141–82   Still trying to cheer the distracted Alonso, Gonzalo tries to move the discussion of government away from the personal problems of the king into a wider context. His choice of the word 'plantation' (l. 141) allows Antonio and Sebastian to wilfully misunderstand him to mean agricultural planting but Gonzalo's utopian vision relates not only to the idea of an ideal commonwealth, but also to the very practical questions of how best to run a 'plantation', that is a colony, thus drawing parallels between this island and the far-off territories the English were beginning to colonize. 'Plantation' was also a term applied to the colonization of a much nearer island, Ireland, by English and Scottish settlers, so the debates here open up a whole range of contemporary political contexts. Gonzalo's speech not only repeats Montaigne's ideas about the nobility of the so-called savage (see Chapter 3, 'The Play's Sources and Cultural Context') but recalls the innocence that Christians associate with the Garden of Eden, and ties in with classical ideas about the Golden Age. However, Antonio and Sebastian undercut it cruelly but not inaccurately by pointing out its internal contradictions: even in this beneficially anarchic world, Gonzalo would be king (ll. 154–6).

Clearly the debate in this scene is an important one for the play, which is much preoccupied with problems of government, self-control, order and anarchy, but it resembles a Platonic dialogue rather than a conversation driven by important social or personal needs, and the fact that Shakespeare puts Montaigne's words into Gonzalo's mouth with very few changes may itself underline our sense that we are watching a staged debate conducted between stage Italians apparently at one remove from the realities of English politics. Yet, as is demonstrated by King James's own writings and the political situation of the early Jacobean period with its many plots (of which the Gunpowder Plot involving Guy Fawkes is the most famous), there are interesting parallels available to anyone who is alert to the nuances of the contemporary political situation. Italy was used routinely as a setting both to emphasize the Machiavellian intrigue of foreign courts and also to provide a useful translucent screen for analysis of the ways of politics closer to home.

By withholding definite identification of Gonzalo until the whole debate about good politics has virtually run its course (l. 168),

Shakespeare encourages his audience to listen carefully in order to be able to discriminate between the different viewpoints and work towards their own identification of good from bad.

183–294 Ariel's entrance (l. 183), playing music, in the middle of the tetchy dialogue between Gonzalo, Antonio and Sebastian, is completely unexpected and, since he has no words, it is explained only by the fact that everyone except Antonio and Sebastian begins to feel sleepy. Prospero has not confided to the audience what exactly his plans for the nobles are, so we are unclear as to what is going on, except that it presumably derives from Prospero's whisperings to Ariel in the previous scene. Since Alonso falls asleep after Gonzalo, and the text is silent on Adrian and Francisco, it would make sense for Ariel to move amongst the nobles, stopping to charm them in turn. Throughout the whole play Antonio and Sebastian offer a negative and corrosive corrective to any expressions of hope or optimism. But it appears to be part of Prospero's plan that they should be given every opportunity to express their true natures. Discounting the fact that they have been shipwrecked, Antonio and Sebastian initiate plots (at line 202) to control Italian towns that they could have no realistic expectation of ever seeing again, simply behaving as though they were still in Italy. The point that their whole enterprise on the island is absurd in context tends not to come out overtly in performance, nor does the fact that their thwarted conspiracy here re-enacts the successful conspiracy against Prospero in Milan but reworks it to a more favourable outcome for Prospero.

Sebastian is named at line 203 and Antonio is finally identified as Prospero's brother only at line 269, thus finally establishing the grid of family relationships and correlating what Prospero has told us about the other characters and their deeds with their own accounts of themselves.

295 to the end When Ariel reappears to save the sleeping nobles, he is again accompanied by music, a characteristic of the magic moments within the play that enhances their sense of otherworldliness. Unusually for him, Ariel addresses the audience directly, in a choric way, before he sings into Gonzalo's ear to wake him. A reader may question why he did not have a similar opening line to 'My master through his art foresees the danger' (l. 295) when he first put the nobles to sleep, and why at the end of the scene he again addresses the audience to tell them that he will tell Prospero what he has done. Critics who try to pin Shakespeare down to having a clearly worked out view of exactly what sort of magician Prospero was and what exactly his powers were over Ariel have some difficulty in explaining such 'lapses', which, of course, tend to pass unnoticed in the theatre. Similarly, in reading, the fact that there would have been no conspiracy here without Ariel's intervention can present a thematically significant but rather different take on Prospero's pre-play failures to confront the conspiracy that ousted him from Milan, since it is Ariel, in some way personifying Prospero's art, who creates the favourable circumstances for renewed conspiracy on this occasion. Although Prospero is not present here, as he will be later in the play, the plot against a ruler is thwarted by his agent, perhaps giving him, at least at a symbolic level, some part of the revenge he craves for the successful plot against him in Milan.

306–25 One of the major functions of this whole scene has been to establish that, while for Antonio and Sebastian it is conspiracy as usual, Alonso has been shocked by the wreck into a state of despair that might make him receptive to some kind of repentance. The actor playing him now has an opportunity to mark the change with a series of speeches that suggest a notably different attitude and tone of voice as he asks questions and gives orders rather than ignoring all attempts to galvanize him. In lines 311 and 314, Alonso's statement 'I heard nothing' and his question 'Heard you this, Gonzalo?' allow the actor and director to develop Alonso's suspicions of Antonio and Sebastian, perhaps emphasizing the pronouns and making it obvious by his choosing to question Gonzalo that he does not trust Antonio and Sebastian, as indicated by his last lines in the scene, where he begins to think it is worth searching for his son, unlike earlier when he was convinced he was dead.

Act II, scene ii

Caliban comes on at the beginning of this scene as Ariel goes off at the end of the previous one, thus creating another opportunity for an almost emblematic moment of contrast. It is not necessary for the two servants to acknowledge or even to be aware of one another, but the audience can be given an opportunity to register the two individuals and to contrast the ways in which they serve Prospero. While Ariel is dealing with conspiracies using music, Caliban is bringing in wood, and there may be a physical contrast between the things they are carrying – Caliban's burden of wood and Ariel's musical instrument – to reinforce the visual comparison. The play has now lasted some 900 lines, very close to half its length, and it has been concerned almost entirely with the dealings of Prospero and his entourage and the Neapolitan courtiers, apart from a brief appearance for Caliban in the middle of a scene involving Prospero's family. A pattern has been established in which Prospero has organized the potential dynastic marriage between Miranda and his old enemy's son Ferdinand. That old enemy, Alonso, has begun to undertake an unexpected crash course in regret and repentance without being aware himself of what is going on. In the light of what has gone before, therefore, we might expect another scene between Miranda and Ferdinand. However, the scene between Caliban, Stephano and Trinculo alters our frame of reference completely. There has been no previous reference to Stephano and Trinculo by name, and their appearance on the island is anticipated only, and virtually subliminally for an audience, by Ariel's brief comment that 'in troops I have dispersed them 'bout the isle' (I.ii.220).

1–14   Instead, Caliban enters with some wood and launches into a virtuoso soliloquy describing the various ways in which Prospero's spirits torment him. The Folio places a stage direction for a noise of thunder at the head of this scene but most editors tend to place it after Caliban's opening rant against Prospero and before 'His spirits hear me' (l. 3), thus motivating Caliban's line. Thus far we are still apparently within the world that has already been established.

14–17   Initially Caliban mistakes Trinculo for one of Prospero's spirits, which initiates another of the play's typical moments of ironic distance between the character's knowledge and the audience's: since Trinculo is a jester he would probably have worn a traditional jester's costume in the original production to indicate his status. Presumably he would also have been recognizable to regulars in the audience as one of the theatre company's resident funny men. Trinculo's costume and the actor's known identity cue the audience as to his likely status, while Caliban has only his insular frame of reference to base his judgements on.

18–40   Trinculo establishes immediately a comic's rapport with the audience, confiding his thoughts directly to them in prose in an immediate contrast with Caliban's blank-verse evocation of the world of night cramps, thus abruptly shifting dramatic registers from courtly tales of revenge and family romance to a much more robust vein of often scatological humour. Trinculo also draws metatheatrical attention to his vision of his environment: it is literally true of the stage that there is 'neither bush nor shrub to bear off any weather at all' (ll. 18–19), but the effect would be slightly different in an amphitheatre or a hall theatre since in the indoor theatre there would actually have been a covering for all the audience and the actors, whereas in an open-air theatre part of the audience would have been fully exposed to the elements. Here, as the actor draws attention to his character's perception of the stage world, thematically linking back to the nobles' debate about their views of the world they have found themselves in (II.i), there are opportunities for by-play with the audience. The actor could perhaps threaten to jump into the auditorium or borrow clothes from someone in the audience, encouraging them to look up to see 'yon same cloud' (l. 23) and failing to notice Caliban until, perhaps, he trips over him.

Together Trinculo and Caliban, and later Stephano, offer comic parallels and contrasts with the main themes introduced earlier. When Trinculo discovers Caliban, it is an ironic recapitulation of Ferdinand's meeting with Miranda, since both of them initially misunderstand what they have just met: Ferdinand believed Miranda was a goddess but discovers she is a maid, while Trinculo thinks he has discovered a fish but then decides he has found an islander. Both see advantages to themselves in their discovery: Ferdinand will marry Miranda; Trinculo will take his islander back home to exhibit him.

Trinculo's successive opinions of Caliban suggest that he tentatively explores him, prodding him with his foot to decide if he is dead or alive, perhaps holding his nose at his fish-like smell or peering under his cloak, at the line 'Legg'd like a man, and his fins like arms', and touching him at 'Warm, o'my troth' (ll. 32–3). As he conducts his reconnaissance of Caliban, Trinculo modulates into a metatheatrical routine as he talks of being in England 'as once I was' (l. 27), telescoping the distance between the imagined world of the play and the world of the audience, as he steps briefly outside that stage world and back into the real world of Jacobean London. When Trinculo states that he could exhibit Caliban as a kind of holiday attraction (ll. 27–32), not only is he glancing at contemporary practices but he is also making a comment on what is going on in the actual theatre: his audience is watching a spectacle in which strange sights are being presented to them in a manner not entirely remote from that associated with the exhibition of Native Americans (see Vaughan, in Hulme and Sherman), so the comment functions in a variety of ways to enhance the audience's sense of the complex layers of illusions in which they are involved.

Trinculo's 'Alas the storm is come again' (l. 36) is an implicit stage direction that motivates his decision to climb under Caliban's coat. He uses a vocabulary calculated to sustain the comic mood as he talks about shrouding himself, and the dregs of the storm (l. 39). There is no actual stage direction as to what goes on but there is plenty of scope for broad physical comedy as the actors try to fight for as much coverage as they can get from the coat, with various parts of each actor emerging at different moments until they eventually reach some kind of accommodation with each other. The gap between the time of their reaching their truce and Stephano's arrival could be quite extended if they decide to have occasional aftershocks, but eventually Stephano enters.

41–54   Stephano is a butler so in the original production he would probably have worn a costume indicating that he was in service to

Alonso, but, initially at least, we have no other idea of who he is. Music is very significant in *The Tempest* but thus far the play's musical protagonist has been Ariel, with songs that are supernatural and ethereal, as we can tell from the contemporary settings for Ariel's 'Full Fathom Five' and 'Where the Bee Sucks' by Robert Johnson, which are reprinted in most editions. However, when Stephano enters singing (l. 41), the nature of his songs is part of the process of dislocation and relocation characteristic of the opening of this scene – much more robust and ballad-like than Ariel's songs, providing a different musical perspective in the play and furthering the major change in atmosphere that this scene is creating.

The actor playing Stephano has clear opportunities for acting drunk, particularly in the transitions between individual sentences. His initial song picks up the notion that rescue is unlikely: dying ashore may be preferable to dying at sea but this is not the best shore to die on. He breaks off, perhaps as the implications of the word 'die' strike him, comments on the song, and has a drink before launching into another, scatological, song, commenting morosely on it and drinking again. Once again there are opportunities for by-play with the audience through grimaces and gestures as he sings and walks (staggers?) about the stage, not noticing Caliban and Trinculo under the gabardine. From Stephano's later comments they must be lying head to toe.

55–84   Caliban and Trinculo may have been squirming throughout Stephano's entrance but eventually Caliban cries out (l. 55), presumably because Trinculo is fighting him for his share of the cover. The cry offers Stephano the chance for double takes, elaborate pantomimic surprise and the full gamut of comedic opportunity, as he readily falls into the same thought patterns as Trinculo did in assuming that the cowering creature under Caliban's gabardine is a man of 'Ind' (l. 58). Stephano's speculations about the situation are punctuated by Caliban's cries of anguish as he and Trinculo continue to struggle, with Caliban still assuming Trinculo is one of Prospero's spirits. Stephano emulates Trinculo in seeing the monster as a commercial opportunity (ll. 66–8, 73–5).

When Stephano approaches Caliban to give him a drink he

presumably approaches the monster, allowing Trinculo to recognize his voice (ll. 83–4), and reminding us that everyone on stage is in some confusion about everyone else's identity.

85–110 When Trinculo cries Stephano's name from the other end of the gabardine it provides more opportunities for comic confusions as well as for puns on defecation that have not stood the test of time particularly well. However, the joyful reunion of Stephano and Trinculo gives us an inkling of the later joys of the courtiers' reunions. To judge from Stephano's complaint 'Prithee do not turn me about; my stomach is not constant' (ll. 109–10), we can get some idea of the boisterous physical reaction of Trinculo to meeting his old comrade, and confirmation of his own state of inebriation.

111–71 Caliban makes a similar mistake to Ferdinand's, taking Stephano and Trinculo for 'fine things' (l. 111) just as Ferdinand initially mistook Miranda for a goddess of the island. At line 113, Caliban says that he will kneel to Stephano but even if he does so at that point, he remains a peripheral figure trying to break into their little circle. While they continue their reunion with excited chatter about their escape they ignored his attempts to join in, as at line 121 where his 'swear' from line 119 is picked up by Stephano but spoken to Trinculo rather than to Caliban. Only at lines 129–30 does Stephano deign to address him. When Caliban is encouraged to swear and 'kiss the book' (line 136), meaning the bottle, we will probably not make a conscious analogy between Caliban kneeling to Trinculo as a god and swearing on his bottle and Prospero's use of his books, but the link is there in the usual form of oath-taking by swearing on the Bible: the knowledge contained in Prospero's books can alter perceptions and change events, just as drinking the contents of the bottle can. Throughout this sequence Caliban is seeking only a new master who will treat him better than he thinks Prospero does, and his offers to serve Stephano echo his complaints against Prospero in Act I, scene ii.

172 to the end The scene ends with raucous singing from Caliban that contrasts with Ariel's delicate singing but also draws a parallel between Prospero's two servants. Both express resentment about being in Prospero's service and stress their demands for freedom, but, whereas Ariel engages in direct rational argument with Prospero and seeks his freedom, Caliban just grumbles and looks for a better master.

Although we are likely to be aware subliminally of the ways in which this scene reflects the play's concerns with matters of government, we are not being asked to tease out family relationships or understand major political issues; we are simply being presented with physical mishaps and misunderstandings. Although it is not clear when the scene ends that it is not an isolated moment of so-called 'comic relief', the suggestion of further plotting by this group of characters holds out the promise of an extended subplot that will thread through the play, offering a typical Shakespearean commentary on themes dealt with more 'seriously' in other strands of the play.

In the next scene we will be introduced to Ferdinand piling up logs, and it is not impossible that when Caliban leaves at the end of this scene he forgets to take his burden of wood, leaving it behind to become one of the logs for Ferdinand on *his* next appearance, reinforcing the sense Shakespeare has already created that Ferdinand and Caliban are oblique reflections of one another as would-be partners for Miranda.

ACT III

Act III, scene i

When Ferdinand appears he is bearing a log, which he may be carrying to join Caliban's discarded bundle, thus offering a possible visual underlining of their status as would-be suitors for Miranda, their subjection to Prospero's will, and their desire to control their own destinies. It is unclear from the Folio when Prospero and Miranda enter but Ferdinand's initial speech is clearly a soliloquy and since Ferdinand has to come on just as Caliban, Stephano and Trinculo go off, if we assume they used two doors, it seems most likely that

Miranda's entrance is delayed until she speaks her first lines. Prospero is also watching this scene but he does not intervene in it, speaking only two asides and the final lines after Miranda and Ferdinand have left the stage.

1–15 Ferdinand's initial soliloquy takes the plot on somewhat since we last saw him and Miranda. Prospero has tried to reduce Ferdinand to the level of his basest servant Caliban by making him take over log-piling but Ferdinand treats his task as in some sense a parody of the tasks a fairy-tale or mythic hero has to perform to win a maiden.

16–31 The way language is used here is a striking example of Shakespeare's capacity for choosing a vocabulary that, while further-ing the plot, also binds the play together through a whole set of shared references to common experience: Miranda's reference to lightning (l. 16) reminds us of the pervasiveness of storms in the play and Ferdinand's reference to sunset (l. 22) also recalls the various expressions of preoccupation with time and the need to complete various tasks (in fact, to perform the play) before nightfall.

31–5 Conventionally Prospero is given an entrance at the same time as Miranda but they clearly do not come on together since she believes he is 'hard at study' (l. 20). There is an underlying irony in Ferdinand and Miranda's belief that they are safe from Prospero's interference when he is present throughout the scene, but it is not at all clear where he is placed on stage. Certainly a proscenium arch theatre could organize the stage picture so that the audience was clearly aware of his presence throughout the scene, but the multiple viewpoints offered by an auditorium such as the Globe's would make this very difficult to arrange in an amphitheatre. It is tempting to imagine Prospero occupying a higher position, in the room above the stage, commanding a view of the situation but equally fading out of the audience's consciousness when he is not directly speaking. Equally, given the young lovers' last words (ll. 90–1), it is possible to assume that they leave by separate exits and that Prospero then comes forward from, for example, the discovery space at the back of the stage. If this were the case then there could be some nice visual contrasts with the later use of that space to discover Miranda and Ferdinand playing chess. If it were also used as Prospero's cell, and perhaps Caliban's 'hard rock', then there could be a useful implicit visual dialogue going on throughout the play, about the kinds of things that happen in the space.

36–7 The fact that Miranda is willing to tell Ferdinand her name is important as an indication of her willingness to make the movement from being her father's child to being her lover's wife. To tell Ferdinand her name is to break Prospero's parental control over her as she, in effect, gives the name he gave her to another man (Caliban, her only other 'suitor', never uses her name). As well as being a disobedient daughter, Miranda is also like a fairy-tale character who gives another person power over her by disclosing her name.

37–74 Ferdinand's declaration of love (ll. 37–48) draws on a prehistory that might be Romeo's, for example, and gives us some sense of the more traditional romantic plot that might have been developed under other circumstances. Interestingly Miranda's reply (ll. 48–59) is not entirely consistent with what she said earlier about having a recollection of women that tended her, nor is her arithmetic consistent with what she said earlier about having seen three men, but although this may be suitable material for textual dispute it is unlikely to affect our viewing of the scene in the theatre. Here the important element in both speeches is the narrowing down of the focus onto the couple, as each, in effect, renounces the potential claims of any other lover. It is noteworthy that Ferdinand has what would later be called 'a past' whereas Miranda of course has none, but also that her modesty (virginity) is the 'jewel in my dower' (l. 54). In this scene Ferdinand and Miranda could be accused of not acting according to what social commentators would have regarded as the most appropriate standards, since they decide to marry without seeking parental approval, even if Ferdinand does think that his father is dead and therefore unable to give his consent (see Chapter 3, 'The Play's Sources and Cultural Context').

74–6   Prospero's aside is interesting because in it he introduces the idea of breeding, metaphorically, when he asks for a blessing on 'that which breeds between 'em'. He is still very concerned that Miranda and Ferdinand might actually begin the physical process of breeding prematurely, so his vocabulary here is almost that of the Freudian slip.

77–91   Prospero introduces a linguistic strand that Miranda follows up unconsciously in 'this is trifling, / And all the more it seeks to hide itself, / The bigger bulk it shows' (ll. 79–81). These lines are usually taken to be a reference to an attempt to keep a pregnancy secret, though they could also refer to sexual intercourse. However one interprets them, they pose a problem for anyone who wants to read Miranda simply as a passive object of adoration: her choice of vocabulary suggests something rather different. Any attempt to create a view of her character has to take account of these lines and they do suggest something rather more interesting than the colourless epitome of virginity that she was sometimes presented as in older criticism and older productions. It may be that these lines simply represent Shakespeare pursuing an image without paying the kind of attention to characterization we would expect of a more naturalistic writer, but it could also be that he is trying to fill out Miranda's character and reduce any sense of her being a nonentity. When Ferdinand uses the word 'freedom' here (l. 89), it links him with other uses of the term by Ariel and Caliban throughout the play, reinforcing the underlying web of contrasts and parallels that are so important in binding it together.

92 to the end   Throughout the scene, Prospero's attitude is quite world weary as though he is disillusioned with his own plans. His choice of vocabulary and the syntax of his direct address to the audience suggest something of the difficulties he has in reconciling his various thoughts and plans:

> So glad of this I cannot be,
> Who are surprised withal, but my rejoicing
> At nothing can be more.   (ll. 92–4)

His use of 'cannot' and 'nothing', coupled with the tortuous syntax, somewhat undercuts any sense of his capacity for rejoicing. Once again he re-emphasizes the real-time aspects of his planning: as Ferdinand has spoken of having to complete his task before sunset, so Prospero must 'perform' (an interestingly theatrical word) much business before suppertime (l. 95).

Act III, scene ii

If Prospero were using an upper space, the change from Act III, scene i, to this scene could easily be effected by his withdrawal from the upper area. If a modern director were trying to stress the sometimes claimed omnipotence of Prospero, this moment of transition would be a good time to underline it by overlapping the two scenes. But equally the gap between scenes that are not using the same acting areas could reinforce a sense of the independence of the two plot strands. Scenes involving Caliban, Stephano and Trinculo sandwich Ferdinand and Miranda's betrothal scene, so there is also a serious contrast here between the drunken lack of inhibition shown by Caliban and his companions and the restraint (chastity) demanded by Prospero of Ferdinand and Miranda. In Act II, scene ii, which in some ways paralleled the first meeting of Ferdinand and Miranda in Act I, scene ii, we had the beginnings of an alliance being formed and there were also links with the ways in which the noble conspirators, both within the staged action of *The Tempest* and in the prehistory of the play, had combined to attack their leaders (Prospero and Alonso).

Presumably the dynamic of the action is one in which Caliban and Stephano occupy one part of the stage, with Trinculo further and further isolated from them as they send him away, but with Ariel standing close by to mimic his voice and create mayhem. Although the impact on an audience is largely comic, the comedy generated here by Ariel imitating Trinculo does link to the play's serious explorations of how identities are formed and why identity confusions are not uncommon on the island.

1–3   Stephano's first speech gives a clear idea of the development of the dynamic of the threesome since he appears to be in mid-argument with Trinculo as they come in (Shakespeare often uses this device to cover an entrance) and he also refers to Caliban as his servant-monster (Ben Jonson picked up on this epithet in some neo-classical jibes at Shakespeare in the Induction to his *Bartholomew Fair*, see Chapter 3, 'The Play's Sources and Cultural Context').

4–39 The initial exchanges between the three comic conspirators demonstrate that they have been very free with the alcohol, offering sharp contrasts with the lack of indulgence that characterizes Ferdinand and Miranda in the previous scene. At line 5 Trinculo suggests that there are only five people on the island (themselves, Prospero and Miranda), thus reminding us of our position of superior knowledge about fundamental issues of a very compartmentalized play. The alternation of scenes throughout the play interweaves different plot strands but the groups of characters remain discrete throughout, with the unravelling of the various plots depending less on any apparent causal interactions than on the dramatist's decisions to take one strand or another forward at any given time (another characteristic the play shares with *A Midsummer Night's Dream*, the only other Shakespeare play that places such sustained reliance on supernatural beings).

The exchanges demonstrate the inconsequentiality of drunkenness as Caliban and Trinculo spar for Stephano's attention, and allow the actors licence to accompany the dialogue with drunken noises, inappropriate pauses, physical unsteadiness and general befuddlement. However, Shakespeare does constantly use parallels in situation and in language to reinforce links across the strands of the play. For example, at line 12 Stephano asserts his own heroism in terms that recall Francisco's description of Ferdinand beating back the waves, in Act II, scene i, but he uses the vainglorious hyperbolic terms of a drunkard to describe himself, whereas Francisco was describing someone else. Similarly, the idea of keeping a good tongue in your head (l. 33) may be proverbial but it also binds the scene to Stephano's discovery of the apparently two-voiced composite monster as well as to the mariners' swearing in Act I, scene i, while the use of the word 'mutineer' (l. 33) and Stephano's threat to hang Trinculo (l. 34) recall the action of Act I, scene i, and Gonzalo's conviction that the Boatswain will die by hanging.

40–84   Caliban kneels to Stephano, pleading his suit like a courtier
in an audience with his ruler. This parodic version of relations
between monarch and subject continues the play's investigation of
what it means to be a good ruler, but in a comic vein. Caliban repeats
his claim that he was the natural ruler of the island and that Prospero
usurped him, thus once more returning to the important theme of
what justifies someone in controlling others: Caliban argues that he
treated the newcomer well and shared his knowledge of the island
with him until Prospero cheated him of his rights by magic.
Prospero, on the other hand, has already given us a version of events
in which the cause of the breach was Caliban's 'natural' (uncivilized)
attempt to rape Miranda. Similarly Caliban remains on the lookout
for a worthy new master and he sees the situation in terms of replaying his initial encounter with Prospero, only with a much more bene-
ficial outcome for himself.

This sequence, with Ariel entering to say 'Thou liest' (ll. 42, 61, 72),
is a classic example of how to use discrepant awareness between the
onstage characters and the audience to comic effect. This scene takes
the comic conspiracy further forward but, as in Act II, scene i, the
development of the conspirators' plans is thwarted by Ariel's intervention. The humour depends very much on the convention that
characters on stage are unable to see another character. We have
already been told that Ariel is to be invisible to everyone but
Prospero, so that and the fact that the other characters do not
acknowledge him would probably be enough to establish his invisibility. This scene resembles the one in which Puck takes on Lysander
and Demetrius's voices in Act III, scene ii of *A Midsummer Night's
Dream*, and Oberon declares himself to be invisible. The surviving
papers of the theatrical entrepreneur Philip Henslowe show that his
company had a conventional way of indicating invisibility in the
form of 'a robe for to go invisible', a useful indication that
Shakespeare may have been anticipating the use of some such device
to underline Ariel's invisibility (Foakes and Rickert, p. 325).

Stephano tries to practise suitable behaviour for a ruler but his
attempts at decorum and appropriate diction are sabotaged by what
he takes to be Trinculo's irreverent interruptions. The stage direction
reminds us of Ariel's invisibility and suggests that Ariel's intervention

is largely verbal, but there are obvious opportunities for sight gags as Stephano and Caliban react to the interruptions and Trinculo is forced to place himself even further away from them. Perhaps too, Trinculo looks for the source of the misleading voice, while being unable to see Ariel, who is in plain sight of the audience and probably very close to him. When Stephano offers to protect his subject Caliban against the depredations of their fellow islander (ll. 67–9), the discourse is framed in terms of crime and punishment that recall earlier aspects of the play, even to the details of Caliban not showing Trinculo where to find fresh water (ll. 65–6).

85–118   Caliban's idea of a plot parallels Antonio and Sebastian's earlier in the play, since the idea is to take the sleeping ruler by surprise, and also, by implication, it reruns the situation of Prospero's original fall from power. Once again Shakespeare uses language that ties the scene in with the rest of the play at the verbal level. At line 85 he picks up on the idea of sleep again (reminding us not only of the nobles' plot but also of Miranda being made to sleep in I.ii) and the importance of Prospero's books (a recurrent thread in the play). The idea of hitting Prospero with a log recalls both Ferdinand's and Caliban's log-carrying, and the notion that Prospero's spirits all hate him has at least some resonances with Ariel's actual complaints within the play. Caliban and Stephano appear to see the scene in ways that parody the familiar concerns of noble marriage: Miranda will be queen of the island, while she and Stephano will found a dynasty. Theatrically, Ariel's presence means that there will be no opportunity for the plot to proceed to a successful conclusion, thus ensuring that the scene is comic rather than serious, since within the play, knowledge is power, and Prospero has supposedly learnt the lessons of his previous failure to keep alert to plots against him.

119 to the end   When the drunkards start to sing and get the tune wrong (suggesting something about their inability to achieve harmony in their attempts at co-operation) Ariel plays the correct tune on a pipe and tabor and they react in characteristic fashion to the invisible music, with Stephano and Trinculo panicking at the phenomenon. Their reaction contrasts sharply with the previous occasion when an invisible Ariel played and sang to Ferdinand. Caliban's reaction is important, however, because he shows us one of the complexities of his characterization with his speech beginning 'Be not afeard, the isle is full of noises' (l. 133). In his speech Caliban demonstrates that he has a sensitive side that does not appear elsewhere in the way he is presented in the play: the music-appreciating, fishlike, would-be-rapist mooncalf is another example of Shakespeare's refusal to go for straightforward caricature and this speech is a key one for those who have developed positive analyses of Caliban's character. One final implicit contrast concludes the scene: whereas previously Ariel's music had led Ferdinand to a positive meeting with Miranda and Prospero, on this occasion it leads the conspirators off stage and distracts them from their purpose of overthrowing Prospero.

Act III, scene iii

The Folio stage direction that begins the scene includes Alonso, Sebastian, Antonio, Gonzalo, Adrian and Francisco and then adds '&c.' However, Francisco has only one line (in response to the appearance of the Shapes, l. 40), and Adrian briefly responds, at the end of the scene, to Gonzalo asking those of 'suppler joints' to follow the distracted Alonso, Sebastian and Antonio, but there are no lines for anyone else, so the wording may reflect the author's initial thoughts about how populated the stage should be. Older editions of the play often added a stage direction that this scene was set on 'another part of the island', but this obscures one of the great flexibilities and strengths of Renaissance stagings: for the audience, temporal absence can translate into a sense of spatial journeying. There is also the visual irony that the nobles have now come back to where they started: that is, the stage, and although imaginatively they have been on a ship and then across the whole island, they have also never been anywhere other than either on the stage or off it. They have been absent since the end of Act II, scene i, for over 400 lines or just under a fifth of the play, during which Ferdinand and Miranda have developed their relationship under Prospero's guidance and Caliban, Stephano and Trinculo have met, got drunk, fallen out and initiated a conspiracy against Prospero.

1–17 The length of time that has elapsed between the nobles' appearances helps the audience to give credence to Gonzalo's claim that they have been creating a maze in their wanderings (l. 2). Nothing has changed substantially from their previous scene except that Gonzalo is tired and the depressed Alonso has again lost faith in Ferdinand's survival, while Antonio and Sebastian, talking privately, and perhaps in hushed voices, are determined to take the first opportunity to pursue their plot (ll. 11–17).

18–52 All this is interrupted by music and Prospero's entrance after line 17. The stage directions indicate that Prospero is elevated above the action. Prospero's presence, invisible to those on stage, according to the stage direction, ironizes the onstage action and he is passive throughout the sequence, simply acting as a choric commentator on the events he has organized.

We cannot be certain about the physical nature of the 'several *strange shapes bringing in a banquet and dancing about it with gentle actions of salutations*' (ll. 19.1–2), other than that they were strange and monstrous but, as the whole history of responses to Caliban within the play suggests, monstrosity is something of a moveable term within the play. The nobles' reactions link back to Trinculo and Stephano's reactions to Caliban, and even to Ferdinand's initial responses to Miranda and hers to him, as they reach for the same kind of vocabulary that Ferdinand, and Trinculo and Stephano, used in reacting to the unknown. They draw on travellers' tales to express the hyper-reality of what they (and we) have just seen, but the audience has the advantage over the nobles since we know that, within a dramatic design that problematizes commonplace ideas of reality, these stage devices are in fact spirits rather than 'real'.

The nobles' responses to the Shapes are differentiated in characteristic ways. Sebastian's 'A living drollery' (l. 21) contrasts with Gonzalo's 'Their manners are more gentle-kind than of / Our human generation you shall find / Many, nay almost any' (ll. 32–4). Sebastian and Antonio are now prepared to believe the more far-fetched travellers' tales that they had previously discredited, yet the audience is aware that these strange apparitions are precisely something contrived and unreal. Gonzalo is always willing to draw moralizing conclusions from the natural world and here he reacts to what he has seen by praising the manners of the Shapes and drawing unflattering comparisons with humankind, offering Prospero the opportunity for a moralizing aside of his own about Gonzalo's companions ('some of you there present / Are worse than devils' (ll. 35–6). Alonso's reaction to the Shapes (ll. 36–9) may be further proof of his developing moral sense, since he reacts to their 'excellent dumb discourse', whereas Sebastian remains resolutely at the corporeal level in simply reacting to the food that has been left behind.

In most cultures the offering and receiving of hospitality has an important set of rules governing who can be offered food by whom, when, and where. Here the Shapes offer food, just as Caliban had shown Prospero the good places on the island and has offered to do the same for his new master. This suggests that the island culture partakes of some of the same rules as polite civilized society. Sebastian's response (ll. 40–2) aligns him with those whose emphasis is on the satisfactions of bodily appetites, but he has transgressed the rules of civilization in usurping Prospero's position, so it follows that he and his fellow transgressors should not be allowed the other benefits of civilization. This means that as they go to the banquet, another special effect, this time consisting of thunder and lightning and Ariel's appearance as a Harpy, destroys their opportunity to eat (ll. 50.1–3).

How Ariel enters like a Harpy is unclear, although it is very tempting to think that it may involve flying. If he did fly in then he may have hovered above the stage or he may have come down to the stage floor, and clearly he has wings that can fold down over the table since he '*claps his wings upon the table*' (ll. 50.2–3). Harpies were a familiar device from classical mythology and Shakespeare may have used an episode in the *Aeneid* – a work that the play echoes on many occasions – when Aeneas and his followers have a feast disrupted by them, as the basis of this moment. Harpies were part bird, part human female, with wings, claws for hands, and female heads. How far this mythological appearance was reflected in the company's costuming is uncertain and it is equally unclear how it ties in with Ariel's sea-nymph costume, if he was still wearing it on his previous appearances. The wording of the stage direction here suggests it may have been written by someone who either saw the effect without knowing exactly how it was achieved, or perhaps had it described to them: *'with a quaint device the banquet vanishes'* (l. 52.3) needs more specific details if it is to serve as a practical stage direction. Many commentators assume that the banquet vanishes through the table and there seems no real reason to dispute what would be an effective and elegant solution. Whether this involves placing the table so that the banquet disappears through a stage trap that the table is placed over or whether the banquet vanishes either into or under the table is unclear but the effect is one still regularly achieved by modern stage magicians. If the noise of thunder and the lightning effects continued during Ariel's entrance, they might have had a practical value in distracting an audience's attention from the machinery of the trick.

There is an effective contrast in this sequence between the harmonious appearance of the Shapes, the quiet discussion of their appearance and then the thunderous interruption of the would-be diners by Ariel's intervention. The symbolism of a thwarted feast is highly significant in showing just how uncivilized the nobles really are. The thunder speaks as a linking thread throughout the play and given its traditional associations with the gods it is highly appropriate as a means of suggesting the influence of supernatural powers on the course of events.

53–82 Shakespeare now begins to reduce the ironic discrepancy between our own knowledge of what lies behind the events on and around the island, and that of the nobles. Ariel reprises Prospero's thwarting of Ferdinand's attempt to draw his sword (l. 60.1) and then invokes the name of Prospero at line 70, and directly suggests that Ferdinand's apparent death is the working out of the slow pattern of retribution. Again the audience is aware that the situation is not as Ariel describes it and the unobserved onstage presence of Prospero undercuts the seriousness of the moment, suggesting, together with what we already know about Ferdinand's actual fate, that there will be a significantly more propitious outcome.

Ariel introduces the idea that what is now going on represents retribution for what had happened to Prospero and Miranda. He makes it clear that there is a choice for the noble conspirators: either they can carry on as before, in which case their fate will be 'lingering perdition', or they can repent their crimes, which will lead to some kind of redemption. What is going on now is an educative and testing process in which the audience is being encouraged to evaluate the nobles' differing reactions to the developing situation. There have been significantly different reactions between Alonso, affected by his son's supposed death, and Antonio and Sebastian, who seem impervious to any suggestion of repentance. The disappearance of the banquet at the end of the speech offers a model of how that lingering perdition might operate, tantalizing the nobles with the possibility of sustenance and then whisking it away as punishment for their past behaviour.

83–93 Ariel vanishes to the accompaniment of thunder at line 82 and the Shapes reappear to carry off the table to the accompaniment of music, reinforcing a sense that this part of the scene is functioning as an anti-masque (see Chapter 3, 'The Play's Sources and Cultural Contexts'). From a modern point of view, the way Shakespeare has organized the end of the scene seems quite awkward: Ariel vanishes in thunder, which could mean that he flies off upwards on the flying apparatus (if that is how he came in), he may descend into a stage trap (thus reinforcing the message of the hellish fate that awaits the unrepentant, and perhaps covered by some kind of thunder-flash effect to accompany the thunder) or he may simply exit through a door under the cover of the thunder effect. However, Prospero, who is on a higher stage level, appears to be speaking to Ariel for at least the first six lines of his own speech (ll. 83–8), which seems quite a long time for a speech to be directly addressed to an Ariel who is not actually on stage. Modern sensibilities might find the idea of Prospero speaking to Ariel as he passes by on the flying apparatus or hangs about on it while Prospero speaks to him equally unacceptable, but there is no compelling reason why Prospero should have moved from his vantage point to join the actors on stage, and editors usually add a stage direction when Prospero leaves, suggesting that Prospero had remained above.

Prospero speaks of his enemies being within his power but gives no clue as to why he leaves them as they are 'knit up / In their distractions' (ll. 89–90), other than his decision to go off to visit Ferdinand and Miranda. Although Prospero is clearly speaking directly to the audience here, he offers us very little insight into his state of mind. After having indulged in some performance criticism, with his praise of Ariel's performance as the Harpy, Prospero then moves on to a statement of the situation rather than an assessment of it. There is clearly a major difference in the way Shakespeare uses direct address to the audience in this play compared with the way that he did in many of his earlier works, both comedies and tragedies, where direct address is often used to give insight into the character's state of mind. At this point Prospero is behaving more like a chorus summarizing the state of the play than as its protagonist. The absence of the kind of insight into a character's thought processes that we find in, say, Hamlet's soliloquies is one of the factors that makes it difficult to clarify what Prospero is actually thinking from moment to moment.

94 to the end It appears that the Harpy was not audible to Gonzalo, who betrays no knowledge of the contents of Ariel's speech to the 'three men of sin'. Alonso has heard what Ariel had to say but he attributes what he has heard and witnessed to natural phenomena: the billows, the winds, the thunder all seem to him to have been the transmitters of the message about his son and Prospero (ll. 95–102), rather than the actual messenger, the mythological figure of the Harpy played by the supernatural figure of Ariel. It is clear that Alonso has begun to feel guilty about his crimes, mainly because of his loss of Ferdinand, but neither Antonio nor Sebastian seems to have any element of repentance as they offer to fight with their tormentors, even if, unlike Alonso, they seem to be acknowledging Ariel's physical presence in the use of the word 'fiend' ('But one fiend at a time, / I'll fight their legions o'er', ll. 102–3). The scene ends with the implicit fault lines in the group beginning to extend even further and Gonzalo is left once again to furnish a choric comment laced with the humour of his inability to get his joints moving ('I do beseech you / That are of suppler joints, follow them swiftly', ll. 106–7).

ACT IV

Act IV, scene i

1–32 Having brought the nobles to the brink of despair, and possibly in Alonso's case self-harm, Prospero abandons them while he pursues his plans for Ferdinand and Miranda with a betrothal masque. Commenting on the early exchanges in this scene (ll. 1–12), critics have expended much scholarly mathematical ingenuity on deciding what the thirds of Prospero's life that he refers to in line 3 really are (or indeed whether he meant a thread) but the general sense is clear: he values Miranda very highly. It is perhaps noteworthy that Miranda becomes increasingly silent as the play wears on. She has almost nothing to say in this scene and only a few, admittedly significant, lines in Act V, scene i. This is consistent with her status as an object of adoration, and once women have been successfully wooed in older drama, by convention they tend to be given very little to say. Prospero explains that his earlier attitude towards Ferdinand was an attempt to test Ferdinand's commitment to Miranda (ll. 5–7), but once again the emphasis on chastity in lines 13–23 has an urgency behind it that actors, audiences, commentators and directors have often felt is under-located in anything that actually happens or appears to be about to happen in the play. Prospero's insistence on chastity is in itself unsurprising; it is part of the common currency of dramatic fatherhood, particularly comic fatherhood. However, Prospero's concern seems to many modern interpreters to lack plausibility and thus to raise questions about his character and what can be seen as the obsessive control that he appears to want to exert over Ferdinand and Miranda. Critics have also pointed to the slightly misogynistic strain of some of the exchanges about Miranda's mother in Act I, scene ii, to show how far derogatory attitudes to women are embedded in the play's discourse. It could be argued in naturalistic terms that Prospero needs to avoid problems with this part of the proposed solution to his dynastic dilemma, such as might occur if Ferdinand seduced Miranda and then rejected her, but it may also be that Shakespeare felt a need to complicate this aspect of the plot. Many responses to the play have focused on Prospero's relative omnipotence in practical matters, so that some kind of difficulty with the courtship could be a useful way of injecting some tension into this strand of the play. Equally this supposed lack of tension may often have stemmed from some of the choices made by directors and actors (particularly in the nineteenth century) that have removed some of the complicating factors by cutting lines that foreground Miranda's sexuality. Ferdinand's response to Prospero (lines 23–31) is couched in suitable terms for a dutiful would-be son-in-law and receives an appropriately paternal response from Prospero.

33–59 Having started as a scene between Prospero and Ferdinand (Miranda actually says nothing at all here), the scene takes off in a different direction as Prospero summons Ariel. In a play of surprises, this scene modulates into the performance of the masque, which is not foreshadowed at all until Prospero mentions his promise to 'Bestow upon the eyes of this young couple / Some vanity of mine art' (ll. 40–1). Prospero has to leave Ferdinand and Miranda to their own devices while he talks to Ariel and it is noteworthy that Ariel's response to Prospero is to modulate into a jingling rhyme on monosyllables creating a long 'o' sound. This type of verse is used in *A Midsummer Night's Dream* and elsewhere in *The Tempest* to suggest magic, but here it leads to Ariel's question 'Do you love me, master? No?' (l. 48), which raises a whole raft of potential questions, particularly depending on such issues as the actual gender of the performer, the supposed gender of the character, the relationship between Ariel and Prospero and whether it is regarded as master–servant (as the choice of vocabulary emphasizes), paternal and familial, or even erotic. The caesura between the two questions in Ariel's line opens up a range of possibilities that can heavily influence how he says 'No', depending on what Prospero is or is not doing at that point, although it could also just be regarded as the necessary culmination of the pattern of rhyming. Prospero's response to Ariel ('Dearly, my delicate Ariel. Do not approach / Till thou dost hear me call,' ll. 49–50) is also open to interpretation as simply the usual response of the harassed father/director faced with doubts from a child or performer. However, Prospero's line can also be played in many other ways, to indicate indifference or regret or longing or any other appropriate emotion, as can Ariel's 'Well, I conceive' (l. 50), one of those typically Shakespearean, apparently simple arrangements of words whose very lack of grammatical complexity can lead to a much more complex set of resonances.

When Prospero turns back to Ferdinand and Miranda from his conversation with Ariel (l. 51), his response to them suggests that the young people may have been forgetting his warnings earlier in the scene. However, once again it is not clear whether his reaction is objectively justified by what had been going on during his conversation with Ariel. The scope for a director here is very wide: the betrothed couple may have been kissing or cuddling or engaged in serious sexual activity; Prospero may be over-reacting to them when in fact they are doing nothing sexual at all, and there is also an opportunity to show differential actions between Ferdinand and Miranda. Ferdinand's response (ll. 54–6) looks very formal and guilty in its stilted quasi-proverbial diction and the piling up of such words as 'white', 'cold' and 'virgin' as qualifiers of snow. Prospero's 'Well' (l. 56), like Ariel's a few lines earlier, can be interpreted in many ways.

60–138   The conventions of the masque play an important role in structuring the events of this scene. Courtly entertainments of an allegorical kind have been quite common throughout history but by the early seventeenth century they had grown in scale and complexity and were attracting major artists such as the architect/designer, Inigo Jones and the dramatist Ben Jonson (see Chapter 3, 'The Play's Sources and Cultural Context'). Shakespeare's company, the King's Men, were sometimes used in these masques and they were certainly used to performing at court. Thus the challenge of writing the masque was of a familiar kind for Shakespeare, although there is no record of him having composed an independent masque. The language of the masque itself is clearly marked off from the rest of the play by the use of couplets, the choice of vocabulary and the formal, rather convoluted use of language, where the build-up of epithets creates a rather Latinate, almost Miltonic, atmosphere. Reversed word-orders create a stiff and hieratic tone that is perhaps appropriate to the theme of chastity and to the way in which the abundance of nature appears to be channelled though the verse form itself as well as through the choice of vocabulary.

The staging involves a significant amount of dancing and music as well as an entrance for Juno by means of a flying apparatus. Since Ariel talks later in the scene about presenting Ceres, it is probable that, as well as having overall responsibility for the masque under Prospero's direction, he also plays this role. We can assume that Juno's entrance involved some kind of representation of her chariot and, although most editors have placed her actual entrance later than the Folio's stage direction, it is possible that she made a slow descent or even that she spent some time suspended in mid-air before finally coming down to the stage floor. It makes sense in terms of modern assumptions about sight lines for Miranda and Ferdinand to be sitting as low as possible, preferably on the floor and with their backs to the majority of the audience with Prospero perhaps off to one side, like the modern Polish director Tadeusz Kantor, watching critically the performance of his protégés.

Unlike in *A Midsummer Night's Dream*, the entertainment is the culmination not of the whole action but of only one thread of it. As we find out, the masque cannot be concluded because the whole plot has not yet fully unravelled. It is premature and its placing in Act IV, scene i, indicates in part that Prospero himself has misunderstood how far his own plotting has yet to go to unravel the knots of the narrative. The masque performs a wide range of functions: first it is, as Prospero suggests, a vanity of his art, meant to entertain the betrothed couple, and its subject matter is in part a reinforcement of his strictures about the need for chastity since Venus and Cupid are evoked verbally but excluded from the action. Secondly, it holds out the promise of a kind of utopian green world of plenty in which the seasons are somehow suspended in a continuum of fertility that is itself the reward for preserving decorum. As such, the masque links back to Gonzalo's musings on the Golden Age in Act II, scene i. It is also a further indication of Prospero's powers over the spirit world and offers a contrast with the storm and with the antimasque-like presentation of the banquet to the nobles: here we have a vision of the creative processes of nature, rather than the apparently destructive forces of the storm and the Harpy scene. Although the goddess

Ceres represents nature we are also aware of the role of the sunburnt sicklemen in the creation of food, another example of the important theme in the play of the inter-relationship of nature and nurture. There is obviously no way of being sure what Shakespeare/Prospero had 'intended' for the unstaged portion of the masque, but what is staged reflects Prospero's concerns about Miranda's chastity, which are expressed through agricultural language at the beginning of the scene, with barren hate and weeds reinforcing the idea of discord, which is subsequently banished from the world of the masque. That world is one in which nature is represented as domesticated, with the powerful and dangerous erotic forces of Venus and Cupid not invited, and nature ordered by the harvesters. While Ceres's comment about the short-grassed green may itself be a metatheatrical reference to actual theatrical conditions, the very idea of a lawn also contrasts sharply with the imagined wild world of the island.

As this is a masque within a play there are none of the opportunities for involvement of the courtiers in the action that characterized real court masques, although, as in *A Midsummer Night's Dream*, Shakespeare allows the onstage audience opportunities to comment on the action at line 118. This exchange includes one of the play's significant textual cruces at line 123; does Ferdinand say, 'wife' or wise'? (It is discussed in Chapter 1 on 'The Text and Early Performances'). The masque ends abruptly in disarray when Prospero recalls Caliban's conspiracy at line 138. In Sam Mendes's 1993 Royal Shakespeare Company (RSC) production he was stirred to this recollection by Caliban actually appearing as one of the sicklemen. Prospero's interruption of the masque breaks up the harmony of the dance and of the music, as the stage direction indicates: at the end of a *'graceful dance'* there is a *'strange hollow and confused noise'* and the reapers and nymphs *'heavily vanish'* (IV.i.138.2–5). In some ways the wording is reminiscent of the kinds of stage directions to be found in printed masques, although there the verbs are usually in the past tense, describing what happened on the unique occasion of the masque, rather than the present tenses of traditional stage directions. The disruption of the masque here is reminiscent of the disappearance of the banquet (which has some characteristics of an antimasque) in Act III, scene iii, and also of the noise that Antonio and Sebastian describe in Act I, scene i.

The abrupt rupture in the apparently serene process of the masque is a pivotal moment in the play. The masque appears to have been intended by Prospero as the culmination of his dealings with Miranda and Ferdinand, but it is too soon in the working out of the whole process of the narrative for it to represent a culmination of the whole dynamic of the play: too much has been left unresolved. This makes for an interesting comparison with the performance of 'Pyramus and Thisbe' in *A Midsummer Night's Dream*, which only takes place after all the main antagonisms have been resolved, when it can offer a parodic recapitulation of the resolved themes of the play. In *The Tempest*, in contrast, Prospero has literally lost the plot at this point and although the masque symbolically banishes the erotically disruptive forces that might disturb Prospero's plans for Miranda and Ferdinand, it cannot offer a resolution to the other plots. When the masque is interrupted we are further made aware that it has been symbolically re-enacting another aspect of Prospero's previous immersion in his magic at the expense of state affairs: just as happened in Milan, he has been distracted from what he should be doing and is in danger of allowing himself to be overthrown by a conspiracy. He is revealed to be not as omniscient as some readings suggest he might be and at this stage his art, both as magician and as dramatic author, is revealed as lacking. The masque does turn out to be precisely a vanity of Prospero's art, and the fact that he has to interrupt it shows that he does not yet control the dramatic action as well as he had believed he did.

139–63 Ferdinand and Miranda are clearly baffled by the turn of events (ll. 143–5). When Prospero redirects his attention to them, he addresses Ferdinand rather than Miranda, with one of the best known speeches in the play, 'Our revels now are ended' (lines 148–58). Although Prospero's speech has been regarded as signifying Shakespeare's renunciation of the stage, it is both perfectly in keeping with the dramatic action at this point and also a reworking of a classical literary theme, so it does not necessarily have some specific autobiographical meaning. The idea that the world is temporary ties in very precisely with the sense that theatrical illusion is created by equally insubstantial means. The comparison of the material world with the creation of theatrical effects is given added force by the idea that what appears to be solid in the real world is in fact as transient as the materials used to create theatrical effects, particularly in the masques. This is a very good example of the concatenation of Shakespearean necessities: Prospero has to provide an explanation of what has just happened and that explanation draws on his art, the fact that he has been indulging in a vanity of that art and the fact that all human experience is ultimately fleeting and baseless. The speech also marks a significant change in his attitude, since he moves from the conventional discourse about the theatre to talk for the first time of his infirmity (l. 160) and perhaps the emphasis on being vexed, weak and troubled at the end of the speech is an indication that his confidence in his art (both theatrical and magic) has been shaken. Clearly, in many ways the collapse of the masque shatters Prospero's own sense of being in control, and reopens the play when it had appeared to be drawing towards a conclusion.

164–9   Shakespeare makes the break between the masque and Prospero dealing with Caliban quite definite: Ferdinand and Miranda leave and Prospero is left on stage alone, a brief emblematic enactment of his isolation from others. In the kaleidoscopic working and reworking of themes, it is now clear that Prospero no longer sees Ferdinand as anything like the same danger to Miranda's chastity that Caliban had been. However, the theme of rebellion remains very significant. Ferdinand and Miranda's exit clears the stage for Ariel's entrance and the defeat of Caliban and his conspirators. When Ariel appears, the relationship between him and Prospero appears in a few deft touches: perhaps Ariel's 'commander' (l. 167) simply means 'you who give me orders' but it is possible to detect a slightly ironic military inflection here. In lines 168–9 Ariel's statement that he held back information from Prospero because he thought it might make him angry is another hint that Prospero's 'serenity' is not unchallengeable.

170–93   The play has a tripartite structure with actions centring on Caliban, the nobles, and Miranda and Ferdinand, and the scenes that take each action forward are temporally dissociated from one another so that when characters reappear there is often a need for a kind of choric summarizing of the situation. Here Prospero's discussion with Ariel (ll. 170–88) seems almost to be reminding Shakespeare himself of where he has got to in the plot, a recapitulation of the story so far. However, this discussion also draws attention to an interesting facet of Shakespeare's dramatic method in terms of the aspects of the story he chooses to show and those that he only tells us about. Prospero needs to be reminded of what has happened to the conspirators but while Ariel's subsequent speech tells us what has happened to them, it is interestingly different from a fairly similar speech in *A Midsummer Night's Dream* where Puck tells Oberon what he has done to the Mechanicals. In the *Dream* the audience has watched the scene that Puck recounts. In *The Tempest* the audience has only seen part of it and the action has been proceeding off stage in ways that Shakespeare has chosen not to dramatize, for unknown reasons. We last saw the conspirators following Ariel off just as he describes (in Act III, scene ii, nearly 300 lines, previously, and before the elaborate staging of the masque), so there is clearly good reason to remind us of what had been happening. However, Ariel takes the story further on from when we last saw him in action, drawing the conspirators on with his music.

The action we have already seen occupies roughly the first part of his speech. He then starts to tell us things that we did not see, including the conspirators' immersion in the pool of standing water by Prospero's cell. Presumably Shakespeare decided against staging the scene that Ariel describes because he needed space for the masque and because he had in mind the antimasque hunting of the conspirators that is to follow. Apart from any practical physical complications involved in staging the ducking, Shakespeare was no doubt aware of the potential comic implications of the arrival of the sodden conspirators and of the visual contrast between their presumably bedraggled appearance and the glistering apparel that Ariel brings out from Prospero's 'house' (we need not assume that there is a significant real-estate difference between Prospero's cell and his house, although the use of the term here may suggest that Shakespeare was thinking of the tiring house as the place where the clothing that will distract the conspirators was located). In saying 'Thy shape invisible retain thou still' (l. 185) Prospero tells us that Ariel is still meant to be invisible, which is a useful reminder, though he has presumably changed back into his sea-nymph costume or a garment indicating invisibility after 'presenting' Ceres, if that actually involved him in playing Ceres himself.

While Ariel is off getting the apparel, Prospero muses angrily on Caliban and explicitly raises one of the play's great themes, the debate about the respective importance of heredity and education in determining an individual's character: 'a born devil, on whose nature / Nurture can never stick' (ll. 188–9). Modern productions tend to interpret the 'line' on which Prospero instructs Ariel to hang the clothes (l. 193) to mean a clothes line, but Shakespeare is almost certainly thinking of the linden tree. This is a useful reminder that what seems like an obvious reading may not always reflect the likely Renaissance understanding, although the many puns on 'line' in the following sequence suggest that some more meanings familiar to us today are also present. If a clothes line is used in a modern production it can be almost anywhere, but on an amphitheatre stage it is possible that a stage column may have done duty for the tree; perhaps the apparel was hung across one of the doors, or perhaps a property tree was called into service.

194–255   Before Caliban, Stephano and Trinculo come on, it is not clear whether Prospero and Ariel have gone off, since there is no exit marked for them in the Folio, although editors usually assume that Prospero and/or Ariel stay on stage. When the conspirators do finally appear '*all wet*' (193.2), they offer a visual parallel with the mariners in Act I, scene i, which may usefully recall subliminally characters who have been completely absent from the action since the very first scene, and prepare us for their eventual reappearance. Since Prospero has just reminded us that Ariel is invisible (l. 85) it would add an ironic visual dimension to the scene if everything the conspirators did was observed by a silent onstage audience, effectively mocking their attempts to keep silent and maintain secrecy. The initial exchanges between the drunken conspirators (ll. 194–213) are a fairly typical drunk scene with much of the comic impetus depending on the ways in which Caliban is trying to enforce silence on his garrulous and sozzled companions, an endeavour undercut at the very least by our knowledge of Prospero's foreknowledge, and in all probability by the visual evidence that they are sharing the stage with Ariel and Prospero. Certainly the dialogue suggests some movement around the stage and Stephano's 'I will fetch off my bottle, though I be o'er ears for my labour' (ll. 212–13) probably prompts Caliban to some kind of action to hold him as he attempts to leave, as well as pointing out that they are near the cell, some 20 lines after they entered (l. 214). Trinculo only notices the 'wardrobe' after that (l. 222). There is obvious comic potential for the conspirators to hush one another, to walk on tip toe, to nearly collide with each other or Ariel and Prospero (if they are on stage) and to indulge in double-takes as they progress towards the cell, presumably walking in some kind of circle from their initial entrance point back towards the discovery space or door representing the cell.

The squabble about the clothes is at one level simply a falling out of drunkards but at a thematic level it enacts one of the key issues of the play by showing how easy it is to be distracted from your purposes by other factors What form the trumpery takes may be important in underlining thematic parallels since once again we have an attempt to overthrow a ruler: perhaps what the stage direction calls the '*glistering apparel*' (l. 193.1) in some way reflects the costuming of Prospero or the shipwrecked nobles in order to underline these parallels. The way the clothes divert the conspirators from their purpose suggests a link with both Prospero's original distraction from the business of good government in Milan as a result of his magic studies, and his very recent distraction from dealing with the various current plots on the island. Caliban is very clear-sighted when he objects to doting on luggage when murder needs to be committed and worries about the dangers of being too late to achieve their ends (ll. 231–2). Caliban however, always the servant, literally ends up again carrying the burden of the scene, as Stephano and Trinculo load him up with garments just before the offstage noise of hunters brings all their plans to nothing.

256 to the end   The wording of the stage direction when the spirit hounds appear ('*Prospero and Ariel setting them on*', ll. 255.3–4) could be taken to mean that Ariel and Prospero had gone off previously and then come on again after the dogs, whipping them on, although, as I have suggested, the sequence works well if they stay on stage throughout it. The conspirators are chased around the stage by actors pretending to be dogs, probably shedding some of the trumpery as they go, while Ariel and Prospero act as huntsmen to the dogs. This sequence is reminiscent of the antimasques which often preceded masque performances and may have been recognizable as such to at least some in the original audiences, particularly at the court performances. Ariel then gives a helpful stage direction ('Hark they roar', l. 261) which suggests that the conspirators have been chased off stage, leaving the space clear for Prospero's summing up. The final speech of this Act (ll. 263–7) is typical of the very flexible verse that Shakespeare is now using, modulating from one thought to another with a vocabulary that tends toward unadorned monosyllables, in which the breaks represented by the use of full stops and commas open up many possibilities of interpretation. The caesuras in 'Shortly shall all my labours end, and thou / Shalt have the air at freedom. For a little, / Follow, and do me service' (ll. 265–7) leave much room for Ariel and Prospero to interact, and Prospero's tone of voice here can open up a range of possibilities (weariness about his labours, and needing to be reminded that Ariel wants to be free; regret that this is what is going to happen; worry about the end).

ACT V

Act V, scene i

Act IV ends with Prospero and Ariel leaving the stage ('Follow and do me service', VI.i.267). Act V begins with both of them on stage again, and, according to the Folio stage direction, Prospero is now in his magic robes. It is highly unusual for Shakespeare to start a scene with those who were on stage for the previous one, and Prospero's opening speech certainly make better sense if we suppose that there has been a significant gap between the scenes. Clearly it does not take very long to put on Prospero's magic robe, although, if we take Act I, scene ii, as evidence, it is helpful for him if he has assistance with the task. One possibility could be that what marks the scenes off from one another is Ariel bringing on Prospero's robes but it does seem much more likely that what has actually happened is that there was an interval between the Acts and that real time has passed as well as dramatic time. If Shakespeare was writing specifically for an indoor theatre, then he would probably have taken account of the necessity of trimming candles, which enforced a structure with intervals on theatre practitioners.

Act V is another lengthy single scene with no change of location, in which Prospero finally brings everyone on the island together, first the nobles, then Ferdinand and Miranda, the Mariners and finally Caliban, Stephano and Trinculo. A major part of the challenge with the final scenes in Shakespeare's late plays is how to manage the necessary series of revelations, denouements and clarifications. Shakespeare was clearly aware of this as, after the real difficulties of staging a whole succession of revelations in *Cymbeline*, he handled the problems of *The Winter's Tale* by sacrificing the staging of the revelation of Perdita's identity in order to give more attention to the survival of Hermione. In *The Tempest* it seems as though Shakespeare has decided to thread Ariel's emancipation throughout the last scene while dealing in turn with partial revelations in the other plot threads. The order is interesting: although he could have simply had Prospero mention that they and the ship had in fact survived the supposed wreck, Shakespeare has decided to bring the mariners back in order to allow his cast to escape the island. However, since we have not seen them since the very first scene of the play, they are potentially anticlimactic. Shakespeare's solution is to bring them in at the end of the more serious reunion sequence and before the broadly comic events involving Caliban, Stephano and Trinculo so that they can fade into the background.

All the action in Act V takes place in the area immediately around Prospero's cell with the revelation of Miranda and Ferdinand playing chess, presumably occurring in the discovery space, where they have some dialogue before moving out to confront the rest of the cast. By the end of the play the stage is somewhat crowded with fifteen people on stage, a group sufficient to give a real sense, for the first time, of a whole society. Previously we have had only isolated groups

together as scenes of division and loss were worked out, but the
increasingly populated stage is a subliminal invitation to hope for
resolution: for the first time in the play everyone is brought together
in one place and for the first time the restlessness that has characterized both the mental and physical states of the characters is stilled.
The dynamic of the scene is one of a movement towards reconciliation, but it is by no means a straightforward process and there is
considerable irony in the working out of the pattern. In particular the
relative silence of Antonio and Sebastian throughout this last scene is
a highly significant element in how the scene is staged, and their
utterances are gnomic enough to leave many questions unanswered.
Further questions are also raised about Prospero's powers and his
intentions, although these will probably be less apparent to an audience than they may be to readers.

1–32 Prospero's decision to wear his magic garment suggests the
seriousness of what he is doing, although it would be hard for us to
try to impose an absolute dress code in relation to his magical activities. He begins the scene declaratively (couched in terms drawn from
alchemy), indicating his confidence now that Caliban has been
defeated, but his questioning Ariel about the time reminds us that the
action of the play is supposed to be taking place in something close
to real time (having supposedly begun at two o'clock and being due
to end by six). Moreover, Ariel chooses to answer the question in a
way that can be played to draw attention to the simmering mistrust
between the characters, particularly depending on the tone of Ariel's
reply and of Prospero's 'I did say so / When first I raised the tempest'
(ll. 4–6). As with the reappearance of Caliban and his co-conspirators
in the previous scene, Shakespeare takes care to remind us of the
status of the nobles before they actually appear, and, as before, Ariel's
account indicates that things have moved on somewhat since we last
saw them. Ariel's vocabulary ('the King, / His brother, and yours', ll.
11–12) reminds us of the importance of family as we move into a
sequence in which families are to be reunited.

Ariel's speeches here, particularly 'if you now beheld them, your
affections / Would become tender' (ll. 18–19) can be crucial in leading
Prospero into his final decisions about the exact form of his revenge.

The play is curiously silent about what Shakespeare planned for the nobles other than Ferdinand. It is possible that he always knew what Prospero was going to do with Alonso, Sebastian and Antonio but chose not to tell us earlier, to preserve some dramatic tension, or it may be that Prospero changes his mind under Ariel's influence. Certainly the idea that Prospero was planning some spectacular physical form of revenge on Alonso at the same time as planning to marry their children to one another does not seem particularly plausible. It seems more likely that what has happened to the court party in the play so far represents Prospero testing the mettle of the three noble usurpers, just as he tests Ferdinand and Miranda as well as the three comic conspirators. This would mean that the outcome of events is determined not by Prospero's will or whim, but by the differing reactions of Alonso on the one hand, and Sebastian and Antonio on the other, to their torments. Of course Alonso is made more susceptible to Prospero's tormenting tutorial by the supposed death of his son and by Ariel telling him in Act III, scene iii, that Alonso himself was responsible for Ferdinand's death because of his own past misdeeds. Nevertheless, Alonso's distraction has led him to repentance whereas Antonio and Sebastian just carried on plotting as always, before they were driven distraught in Act III, scene iii.

Prospero responds to Ariel's suggestion that if Prospero saw the nobles, his affections 'Would become tender', with 'Dost thou think so spirit?' (l. 19). This exchange can be particularly significant in terms of how the actor playing Prospero chooses to interpret the lines: it could be a genuine surprise, carried on when he responds to Ariel's reply ('Mine would, sir, were I human', l. 20), that something so clearly inhuman should be more humane than he was prepared to be, or it could represent some confirmation of what he already thought but had not yet expressed to the audience. In any case, this is clearly the moment when the play settles one of its generic conundrums: it may deal with potentially tragic actions but it is not a revenge tragedy in any conventional sense since Caliban's revenge is thwarted and Prospero's revenge now culminates in both forgiveness and the union of the two noble houses. Prospero's diction here suggests that his magnanimous response is hard won: monosyllables predominate both in his initial reply to Ariel and at the beginning of his next speech (ll. 20–32), and only gradually do the verbs and nouns acquire qualifiers; Prospero may even be groping for words as he tries to formulate his feeling since Ariel has a 'touch' and then a 'feeling' of their afflictions, as Shakespeare sets up contrasts between the insubstantial character and the suggestion of physical contact in the words 'touch' and 'feeling' (l. 21). As Prospero struggles towards forgiveness via proverbial wisdom, meanings cram in with the choice of words such as 'kindlier' (l. 24), which means both 'more kind' and 'more in keeping with being human' (as in human kind). Thoughts continue across lines, and caesuras suggest stages in the thought process until the conditional 'They being penitent' (l. 28). This means 'if they are penitent', then I will forgive them, but at first hearing it will sound like a statement of fact. However, Ariel has referred only to Alonso's penitence and we shall see that things are very much more ambiguous with Antonio and Sebastian.

33–50   There is a stage direction later in the scene (l. 57) that indicates Prospero has made a magic circle, so he must do this at some point before Ariel brings the nobles on. This seems like a suitable moment.

Once Prospero has reached his decision and Ariel has gone off to fetch the nobles, Prospero launches into a magnificently oratorical invocation of his spirits. This speech is closely derived from one by the witch Medea in the Roman poet Ovid's *Metamorphoses* (Shakespeare appears to have been familiar with the original Latin as well as the standard contemporary translation by Arthur Golding; see Chapter 3, 'The Play's Sources and Cultural Context', for a fuller discussion). Although it will probably not be noticeable in production, the invocation ends without a main verb, so the precise meaning of the speech is never fully determined but rather is suspended forever in a grammatical limbo as Prospero abjures his rough magic. The content of the speech is also problematic if it is subjected to close scrutiny, since Prospero's claims here are not entirely consistent with what appear to be the limits of his magic within the play. In particular, his claim to be able to resurrect the dead suggests a far greater control over nature than he actually manifests in the play, and raises some complex questions about black magic and white magic.

However, in production the fact that Prospero has created a storm by his power and has employed spirits to present the banquet and the masque and to hunt Caliban, Stephano and Trinculo lends credibility to this final rhetorical flourish. The importance of the speech lies precisely in giving us a sense of what it is that Prospero is now choosing to give up in favour of a less exalted type of power. In some ways the speech is still slightly premature, since it anticipates his resignation of powers and, although this will be confirmed in the epilogue, he does not specifically break his staff, or drown his book, within the text of the play. Presumably the speech is placed here because a later invocation would be harder to manage with the increasing number of people who will come to populate the stage as the scene progresses. The speech is divided into two parts: one, the invocation, is full of references that emphasize the potency of Prospero's art, but in a single line he converts all of this potency into a 'rough magic' (l. 50), suggesting his own awareness of precisely those limitations of mortal power that the action of the play has suggested, and also of the hyperbole of his immediately preceding claim to raise the dead.

50–7 The second part of the speech is much more practical, and stage-managerial rather than magus-like or magisterial. Once Prospero has abjured his magic, we get lines that suggest the practicalities of the theatre as much as anything else: 'when I have required / Some heavenly music – which even now I do' (ll. 51–2). This points up exactly the parallel between magic and stagecraft: Prospero the magician is calling on spirit musicians; Shakespeare the author is providing a very clear cue to the actual musicians in the theatre that it is time to get ready to play. Whether 'heavenly' refers both to the nature of the music (described in the subsequent stage direction as '*solemn*') and to the location it is played in (the so-called 'music room' above the stage in the amphitheatre) is open to conjecture, but it would certainly be highly appropriate if the source of the sound was hidden from the audience.

The wording of the stage direction that indicates Prospero has made a magic circle indicates that he must have done this at some point before Ariel brings the nobles on, and suggests that he has left some physical trace of that circle, into which the nobles can step.

Whether the circle is actually chalked on the stage or simply indicated by Prospero drawing his magic staff in a circle is unclear. The
stage management of this scene will have to be carefully organized so
that the full visual impact can be achieved, and the nobles will need
to be spaced out so that Prospero can move round them addressing
each in turn. According to the stage direction, Alonso, Antonio and
Sebastian are united by 'frantic gesture' but form two groups, Alonso
'attended by Gonzalo', Sebastian and Antonio 'attended by Adrian
and Francisco' (ll. 57.2–4).

58–87   As so many times before in the play, Prospero observes a
group of characters on stage. In this case the music he has called for
is both therapeutic and in some way a means of dissolving the charm.
It is not clear when the music is supposed to stop and it may be used
mainly as a cover for the nobles' entrance, finishing after Prospero
has commented on the value of music in dealing with the after affects
of trauma, or it may play on for some time, perhaps changing in
volume to background sound as Prospero addresses the nobles,
perhaps modulating to accompany Ariel's subsequent song (ll.
88–94) and then stopping.

   As Prospero continues to speak, not only does he place each of the
nobles for us in a hierarchy of his responses to them, but he also gives
clear indications of how they should be reacting as the charm
dissolves. Noticeably he starts with Gonzalo, for whom he has nothing but good feelings, before moving on in descending order through
Alonso and Sebastian to Antonio, drawing attention to their current
suffering, using a vocabulary that explicitly links the civilized savage
with the uncivilized savage through the choice of 'pinched' (l. 74) and
'pinches' (l. 77), with the difference that, unlike Caliban's, these
pinches are inward. Prospero also stresses the unnaturalness of
Alonso, Sebastian and Antonio's acts, another contrast with Caliban,
whose nature is unaffected by nurture whereas theirs was supposed
to be improved by civilization. To an audience, Prospero's lines to the
nobles will have the force of direct accusation and of forgiveness but,
as he says, there is 'Not one of them / That yet looks upon me, or
would know me' (ll. 82–3), so we have to take his commentary for the
act rather than observe any interaction at this stage. When Prospero

decides to change his clothes again, he intends to confront the nobles not as the magician but as Duke of Milan, asserting his temporal authority rather than his magic power through the symbolism of donning his hat and rapier and by discarding his magic robe (ll. 82–7).

88–103 Ariel's song looking forward to his freedom suggests his joy at his imminent release, and the stage picture of him performing another service while he sings of freedom can be almost emblematic of his relationship with Prospero, as Prospero recognizes with another promise of freedom, and then the line ends with the enigmatic 'so, so, so' (l. 96). What these repeated words indicate is unclear: perhaps they refer, as Orgel thinks, to Prospero sorting out his clothing; perhaps they are some form of regret and acknowledgement of the changing relationship between Prospero and Ariel; perhaps they indicate that Prospero is working out the sequence of what should happen next since he then instructs Ariel to bring the mariners, who have not been heard of since Act I, scene ii, to join the party. The interpretive choice seems to be between something pragmatic motivating the words or something more emotional and/or intellectual.

104–25 Gonzalo, as befits his unproblematic status as Prospero's friend, is the first to emerge from the spell, still disorientated and ignored by Prospero, now in his full Duke of Milan outfit, who confronts Alonso. Throughout the play Prospero has been usually seen in isolation and he does not have to make much physical contact with anybody, except possibly when Miranda helps him off with his magic robe in Act I, scene ii, and then tries to intercede on Ferdinand's behalf later in the same scene. He may also tender Miranda to Ferdinand by giving him her hand, in Act IV, scene i. On other occasions a director and an actor may choose to make his relationship with any or all of Ferdinand, Miranda, Caliban and Ariel physical but there is very little evidence to suggest that he has to have physical contact with anyone. This physical isolation can be an important factor in creating the role and there is certainly no necessity for him to embrace anyone, before he does so to the bewildered Alonso (l. 109). This embrace seems important both because of the scarcity of previous physical contact between Prospero and the other characters and also because it literally embodies his sense of the need to be touched and to feel other examples of humanity. It can also be a comic moment, because poor Alonso is still emerging from his enchantment, so may well not react kindly to being grabbed by someone he can only just recognize as Prospero. Unsurprisingly, therefore, there is a strong sense in Alonso's speech of insisting on the corporeal as he checks Prospero's pulse (l. 113). He, like Ferdinand, is one of Prospero's successes because he immediately resigns the dukedom to him and asks for his forgiveness (ll. 118–19). It is a mark of the difficulty of orchestrating this kind of scene that Prospero then turns immediately to Gonzalo, again indicating physical contact in his desire to embrace him (ll. 120–1). Prospero overtly greets the nobles as 'friends all' (ll. 125), suggesting perhaps some brief encounter with Adrian and Francisco before his confrontation with Antonio and Sebastian.

126–34 The surprisingly brief exchange with Antonio and Sebastian seems to be a private conversation since Prospero specifically tells them that he will not inform on them to Alonso. One of Prospero's key failures appears to be that he has not succeeded in changing the ways in which Antonio and Sebastian behave: Antonio says nothing here and Sebastian only 'The devil speaks in him' (l. 129). Orgel regards Prospero's 'No' in reply as very weak but it could be monosyllabic in its hardness, accompanied by a reminder of Prospero's magic powers, and it could also be an indication that Prospero is no longer impressed by Sebastian's bluster. When Prospero turns to Antonio the confrontation lacks the reconciliation which characterized the meeting of Prospero and Alonso and there is a clear sense syntactically of Prospero's struggle to forgive him (ll. 130–4). Interestingly, Antonio says nothing at all when Prospero requires his dukedom back.

134–71 Alonso's 'If thou beest Prospero' (ll. 134 onwards), with its request for details of how everything has come about, will usually be seen as Alonso breaking away from the other group to interrupt the ongoing confrontation between Prospero, Antonio and Sebastian. It could, however, also be played as a necessary intervention if Antonio appears to be about to not play by the rules of Prospero's game. Perhaps the shared half-lines between Prospero and Alonso at line 134 could include a silence of Pinteresque proportions between Prospero and Antonio as the two brothers confront one another in another battle of wills, before Alonso finally completes Prospero's line. Certainly there is nothing in the scene to give us any guidance that everyone is actually reconciled, since Antonio has only one more line, a comment on Caliban, Stephano and Trinculo. His silence may or may not speak volumes yet it does seem slightly odd that one of the play's key antagonisms should be left dangling in this way. It is not uncommon for dramatists to do this (and Shakespeare himself, for example, does not give us a verbal clincher to sort out Isabella's response to the Duke in *Measure for Measure*, which is a similarly important element in how we are meant to understand the ending of that play), but directors sometimes handle the resolution of fraternal conflict silently here, perhaps with some gesture of reconciliation as the nobles go off to the cell at the very end of the play.

Alonso's intervention brings us to the big moment in which the two royal families are restored and reunited. Alonso is doing exactly what Prospero wanted when he talks of Ferdinand and Miranda as king and queen of Naples (ll. 149–50) without any prior suggestions from Prospero, and thus the way is clear for the final revelation that will clinch the dynastic deal. Prospero's final speech before discovering Ferdinand and Miranda could be an example of him (or perhaps Shakespeare) playing with his audiences as he switches from his discussion with Alonso about lost children to draw attention once again to the other dazed lords, using the occasion to reinforce the message about who he is and what has been going on, contrasting his island experience with the world of the court through an express comparison of his current circumstances with the usual expectations of what a court should be (ll. 153–71). The pun on Miranda's name in 'bring forth a wonder' (l. 170) confirms Prospero's enjoyment of his manipulation of events.

Prospero then moves, probably to the back of the stage, to discover Miranda and Ferdinand, presumably by drawing a curtain that has previously hidden them from view. One of the reasons for the discovery taking place at this stage of the denouement, rather than as the culmination of the whole scene, would seem to be that it would be easier to organize the stage picture with fewer people than will eventually crowd the stage space when Caliban, Stephano, Trinculo and the mariners have all arrived. Given that the discovery would have to take place at the back of the stage, it is presumably important that as many audience members as possible should see it.

172–215 One of the play's many ironies is that the presentation of Ferdinand and Miranda playing chess sits oddly with the idea of harmony that critics and directors have often encouraged us to see at the end of the play. Chess is not now the most obvious thing to associate with young lovers, nor is playing it the most obvious to demonstrate their co-operation and affection. There does appear to have been some suspicion in the period that playing chess was used as a cover for sexual assignations (somewhat later the dramatist Thomas Middleton would use chess in this way in *Women Beware Women*), so there may be period connotations that escape us. Clearly there are political elements in Ferdinand and Miranda's impending marriage and perhaps chess offers a way of regularizing and codifying the political issues that underlie the action (Middleton would use the game to convey political messages in *A Game at Chess*). In this context Miranda can accuse her lover, the son of the man who deposed her father, of cheating (l. 172) and then excuse him readily even if he was fighting unfairly with her for the control of twenty kingdoms (ll. 174–5). Perhaps an audience is most likely to see this moment as symbolizing that the political struggles between the two families have been reduced to a game that channels them into a set of agreed rules and conventions.

The reactions of the onstage audience are significant: Alonso, as we would expect, is delighted that his son is alive but wary that this may be yet another trick, whilst Sebastian is given the line 'A most high miracle' (l. 177). This line seems like one that would be appropriate for Gonzalo, but later in the scene he specifically excuses his silence at this point by saying that he was overcome by emotion. Thus, the line does seem to be correctly assigned to Sebastian, but it is hard to work out whether he means it, in which case he has apparently undergone a very sudden change of heart, or whether he is just carrying on being sarcastic. He has nothing else to say on the subject, although his only later remark in the play does not suggest that he has been particularly imbued with a sense of happiness.

Ferdinand and Miranda's response to their discovery is to do what characters in discovery spaces usually do, which is to get out of the backstage area into the main acting areas as soon as possible: Ferdinand comes forward to kneel to Alonso, who embraces him, while Miranda speaks her most famous lines, welcoming the 'brave new world / That has such people in't' (ll. 183–4). Given the composition of the group of people on stage, Prospero's immediate corrective ('Tis new to thee', l. 184) reminds us that this beauteous world is in fact populated by usurpers, both actual and potential, and would-be murderers. Clearly there is considerable irony in these moments and Miranda's lines are often directed towards Antonio and Sebastian in order to underline that irony. Alonso, like Ferdinand, initially thinks Miranda is a goddess but is soon disabused and the scene moves to a close after some brief explanations, with Gonzalo offering some choric rationalizations of the whole process, in which he makes the point about the metaphysical nature of the voyages of discovery that they have undertaken. He includes everyone in this encomium, but the silence of Sebastian and Antonio still leaves room for them to indicate their own lack of inclusion by gesture and posture. Perhaps there is something of an indication of this in Alonso's blessing on Ferdinand and Miranda: 'Let grief and sorrow still embrace his heart / That doth not wish you joy' (ll. 214–15). Gonzalo's 'Amen' provides a suitably solemn finale for this sequence.

216–55 Prospero's guiding role becomes ever more obvious as he drip feeds more characters onto the stage, and the focus changes as Ariel enters with the Boatswain and the Master 'amazedly following' (ll. 215.1–2). Bringing the sailors back on stage here reminds us of the first scene and, in Gonzalo's reaction to them (ll. 216–20), once more foregrounds the themes of governance and control that were raised in that first scene. One of Alonso's character notes in Act V is an attempt to make sense of what has happened on the island in a way that is characteristic of senior figures in Shakespeare's plays (the Prince in *Romeo and Juliet*, for example) but he is thwarted by his imperfect knowledge (ll. 242–5). Prospero sooths him with a promise to explain everything, but his dealings with Alonso remain generalized and opaque, encouraging him not to try to make sense of events until Prospero is willing to tell him what has actually happened, and 'till when, be cheerful / And think of each thing well' (ll. 250–1).

256–318   Prospero has one more set of rabbits to bring out of his hat as Ariel brings in Caliban, Stephano and Trinculo 'in their stolen apparel' (l. 255.2). There are visual possibilities here to use similarities between their clothing and Antonio and Sebastian's to underscore the parallels between educated and natural savages. Stephano's initial words, clearly not addressed to the onstage assembly, recall the traditional shipwreck cry of 'every man for himself' but, as before, his drunkenness means he gets it wrong, in this case in a way that is highly appropriate to one strand of this scene: 'Every man shift for all the rest, and let no man take care for himself' (ll. 256–7). This may not be what he intended but it comes close to being one of the play's central concerns and it is typical that Shakespeare should undercut it by putting it in the mouth of a drunkard. Trinculo's opening words echo Miranda's response to essentially the same group of people as he picks up her use of the word 'goodly' ('how many goodly creatures are there here'; 'here's a goodly sight', ll. 182, 265). Few audience members will overtly associate Miranda and Trinculo yet their shared vocabulary can help to open up a series of cross-connections between characters and situations to the enrichment of the whole play.

Caliban is suitably awed by Prospero's physical appearance as befits someone who operates mainly on the material level ('How fine my master is!', l. 262), unlike Antonio and Sebastian who continue to behave as though nothing much has changed in their world or in their outlook, with an exchange considering the market value of Caliban and his companions (ll. 264–6). Antonio comments that Caliban, who he has just seen for the first time, is 'a plain fish, and no doubt marketable', l. 266). Antonio and Sebastian's discussion about marketability is entirely consistent with their general approach throughout the play, and thus a reminder of Prospero's inability to change their minds, but, taken with the reference to Caliban as a fish, links them very much with the low comic characters who made the same initial assessment of Caliban. The comparison is not to Antonio and Sebastian's advantage, and an audience is likely to regard the ineptly serious plotters less sympathetically than they do the comic conspirators, who have at least been the cause of our laughter. But Prospero must admit that he takes some responsibility for Caliban, just as the other nobles are responsible for the butler and the jester. Sebastian continues to be resolutely prosaic, wondering where Trinculo managed to find wine, but Alonso converts essentially the same question into a much more poetic image (ll. 279–80). Perhaps this contrast will serve to underline the difference between them, albeit it will probably only be picked up subliminally by an audience, just as the network of cross-references throughout the scene and indeed the play will for the most part operate implicitly rather than overtly. A shared word here, a shared posture there, a shared reaction and a different response can all be used to underpin and reinforce the overt action. Similarly, when Prospero asks Stephano if he would be 'king o'the isle' (l. 287) there will be other characters on stage who are equally guilty of plotting to overthrow legitimate rulers. As Caliban feared, he is indeed punished but only by being asked to trim Prospero's cell, and clearly there is a difference between his ready consent and the refusal to acknowledge his crimes which still characterizes Sebastian. Sebastian's last words in the play cap and correct Alonso once more as though he cannot give up his position of assumed linguistic superiority (l. 299).

The intractability of Sebastian and Antonio here is important for the overall meaning of the play because it severely undercuts any suggestion that the mood is one of unproblematic reconciliation; we simply do not have enough evidence to make such a judgement. Although we should be careful not to read ambiguities into silences where none may be present, it is striking that Shakespeare finds room for the mariners but not for some words of repentance from Antonio and Sebastian. The ending of the play is ambivalent enough to make some later writers speculate on the question of what happens on the return voyage (see Chapter 6, 'Critical Assessments').

Ariel does not have an exit marked after he drives Caliban and his fellow conspirators on at line 255 so he may be on stage for

Prospero's final instruction (ll. 316–18), sometimes with interesting results in terms of his response to being given his freedom (see Chapter 4, 'Key Productions and Performances'). Prospero does not reveal Ariel to the assembled cast in Act V, so that the characters remain ignorant of his guiding role in the events on the island. This dramatic irony remains until the end, with the audience in possession of many more facts than the majority of the cast. Prospero's final comment to the onstage audience, 'Please you draw near' (l. 318), serves to take them off to clear the stage for his Epilogue. How exactly the exit is organized may yet allow a determined director to find reconciliation in some form of acknowledgement from Antonio and/or Sebastian, to Prospero.

319 to the end Commentators have often suggested that this Epilogue is unique in Shakespeare in that Prospero does not come out of character (as, for example, in the Epilogue of *All's Well that Ends Well* when 'The king's a beggar now the play is done') and it is unusual in that it is spoken by Prospero himself, rather than by the actor playing Prospero, but it does share some characteristics with Puck's Epilogue in *A Midsummer Night's Dream*, where the magical spell is to be concluded by clapping. In *The Tempest* something similar is going on: part of the Epilogue is a conventional plea for applause but the audience must also engage with the whole process of Prospero's actions by not withholding their applause and 'Gentle breath' (l. 329). Prospero/the actor playing Prospero plays on the idea of the actor's art and the magician's art, modulating from one to another and in some sense stressing but also denying the duality of actor/character since, as Prospero has foretold, we are all actors. The speech is in rhyming couplets, which itself distances us from the usual mode of Prospero's discourse, but even so, the stress in the last part of the speech on despair, prayer, mercy, crimes, indulgence and pardoning suggests something that moves beyond a simple plea for applause into a more direct contact with the audience's hopes and fears. And interestingly, 'indulgence' puns both on our modern sense and on the much older (and Catholic) sense of an indulgence which gives 'remission of the punishment for sin' (Orgel, note to V.i.338).

3 The Play's Sources and Cultural Context

Shakespeare wrote *The Tempest* at a time of major intellectual and physical exploration. Although the play has no direct sources, in the sense that *Romeo and Juliet* has in being taken from a work by Bandello via Arthur Brooke, or that the Roman plays and the English history plays have, being taken from Roman historians and English chronicles, Shakespeare was influenced by a wide variety of materials and drew on a vast body of literary texts and folklore including both factual and fictional accounts of voyages and shipwrecks in many genres and from many cultures, as well as stories of magic and supernatural beings, philosophical speculations and the news of the day.

The play has been variously categorized as a Romance, an Epic and a Pastoral and generically it certainly is indebted to all of those forms. Theatrically it uses elements associated with the court masque and the newly fashionable genre of Tragicomedy, and adopts a neo-classical approach to the Aristotelian Unities that varies considerably from Shakespeare's own normal practices. The play also draws on contemporary news in the form of the particularly sensational real-life story of the shipwreck of the *Sea Venture* and the recovery of its crew. Shakespeare drew on accounts of contemporary voyages as well as debates about power, government, ideal commonwealths, the nature of magic, proper behaviour within the family, and the duties and rights of princes. Some of these varied debts can be traced directly in Shakespeare's use of specific motifs or even, in a few cases, actual speeches from other literary works; some of these debts are verbal, some are situational, some are tonal or thematic, and some are so closely integrated into the structure of events that, although they permeate the whole texture of the play, are almost invisible to a modern eye. In this section I discuss some of the more important aspects of those intellectual and cultural contexts and reproduce some contemporary documents that exemplify them.

The sea and travel

London, a relatively small town by modern standards, was founded on trade, particularly ocean trade, and there is a range of evidence that shows how far and how directly contemporary society was influenced by maritime adventures and particularly the 'discovery' of America: Francis Drake circumnavigated the globe in 1577–80; Walter Ralegh bought back two 'Indians' from his 1585 expedition to Roanoke Island; there was an extensive travel literature such as Thomas Harriot's *Briefe and True Report of the New Found Land of Virginia* (1588); Captain John Smith's famous encounter with Pocahontas took place in 1607 and he returned to England in 1609; John Rolfe, who eventually married Pocahontas, and took her to England in 1616, was a passenger in the *Sea Venture*, which was lost off Bermuda in 1609. The wreck of the *Sea Venture* and what happened to its crew was very important to the genesis of *The Tempest*.

There is ample evidence of Shakespeare's general interest in the voyages of exploration, and trade, to America and the West Indies. For example, he mentions travellers' tales in *Othello* as well as *The Tempest*, he refers to a ship going to Aleppo, in *Macbeth*, and also jokes about cartography in *Twelfth Night* when Maria refers to Malvolio smiling his face 'into more lines than is in the new map with the augmentation of the Indies', probably a reference to a map published in *The Principall Navigations, Voiages, Traffiques and Discoveries of the English Nation* (1598–1600), compiled by Richard Hakluyt.

Shakespeare also drew on his reading and aspects of the common stock of narrative motifs that go back to Homer: stories of shipwreck, separated families and disastrous voyages can be traced back to the *Iliad* and the *Odyssey*. Amongst Shakespeare's earlier plays, shipwrecks figure prominently in *The Comedy of Errors* and *Twelfth Night* (where Sebastian shares a name with a character in *The Tempest*), and among his later ones, in *Pericles* and *The Winter's Tale*. Shipwrecks obviously function as an economical way of distributing characters in unexpected places at unexpected times and one should not forget that without modern methods of construction, communication and navigation, the likelihood of ships being lost without any clear explanation of the circumstances was very much higher than it is today: in *The Merchant of Venice* we are told that Antonio (another name that reappears in *The Tempest*) has lost ships that then turn out to be safe, which is precisely the kind of situation that happens in the fictional world of *The Tempest* and that happened in real life with the crew of the *Sea Venture* in 1609.

The *Sea Venture* and the Virginia colony

When the rest of the flotilla the *Sea Venture* was sailing with to the Virginia colony lost sight of the ship in a very bad storm in 1609, it was assumed that both ship and crew had been lost. However, the crew actually managed to reach shore in the Bermudas (which up till then had been regarded as a particularly hostile environment) and eventually built smaller ships from the wreckage, which they then sailed on to Virginia, their original destination. Reports that had reached London about how badly things were going with the Virginia colony had led to the Virginia Company (which was responsible for the enterprise) publishing a pamphlet to try to refute those claims. Apparently *A True and Sincere Declaration of the purpose and ends of the Plantation begun in Virginia* (1609) did not achieve its aims but the startling news that the *Sea Venture*'s crew had survived reached London in 1610 and Sylvester Jourdain, who had been on the ship, published his *Discovery of the Barmudas* in October. William Strachey's long letter about the wreck and subsequent events reached England in September 1610 but was not published until 1625, under the title *A true Repertory of the wrack and redemption of Sir Thomas Gates, Knight*. The Virginia Company issued *A True Declaration of the state of the Colony in Virginia with a confutation of such scandalous reports as have tended to the disgrace of so worthy an enterprise* in late 1610. Although the exact circumstances that led Shakespeare to a detailed knowledge of the so-called Bermuda pamphlets are not clear, most of the material was published and therefore readily available when Shakespeare wrote *The Tempest*. Although Strachey's letter was not published until after Shakespeare's death, he appears to have been well acquainted with it, since there are both verbal parallels and signs that his treatment of the narrative in the play owes some of its tone to Strachey's view of the actual wreck and its aftermath. There is no direct proof that Shakespeare knew Strachey personally, but there is a considerable body of evidence that links Shakespeare to the Digges family, who were heavily involved in the Virginia Company, so he may have read Strachey's letter under their auspices and he may have actually known Strachey, who had had business connections with the Blackfriars theatre at one point.

Clearly the Bermuda pamphlets as a whole point to some of the main elements of *The Tempest*: shipwreck and survival against the odds, providential outcomes, thwarting of mutinies, questions of government, and the ability of the apparently fearsome islands haunted by spirits to sustain European humankind. Some of the topographical details match those in *The Tempest*, although any travel narrative is likely to supply similar discussion of climate, flora and fauna.

Of course the shipwreck in *The Tempest* occurs when the ship is on a voyage from Algiers to Italy and the play's action therefore takes place on an island somewhere in the Mediterranean between Algiers and Italy, but the references in the play to Bermuda and to Indians locate its imaginative world in the spirit of exploration. Furthermore, the idea that the running of a ship equated metaphorically with the running of a government is neatly encapsulated in the idea of the ship of state, a concept developed as early as Plato, which is raised in the first scene of *The Tempest* and implicitly underlies its whole treatment of the question of good government.

The *Sea Venture*

These extracts from three of the contemporary documents about the wreck of the *Sea Venture* and the Virginia colony demonstrate

Shakespeare's indebtedness to them for both specific incidents and the general atmosphere of *The Tempest*, not only in the wreck scene but also in his delineation of aspects of the island and some of the arguments on it.

Extracts from *A true repertory of the wrack and redemption of Sir Thomas Gates, Knight, upon and from the islands of the Bermudas, his coming to Virginia, and the estate of the colony then and after under the government of the Lord La Warre. July 15, 1610, written by William Strachey, Esquire,* **from** *Purchas his Pilgrimes* **(1625)**

[The storm and the wreck]

[T]he clouds gathering thick upon us, and the winds singing and whistling most unusually . . . a dreadful storm and hideous began to blow from out the north-east, which swelling and roaring as it were by fits, some hours with more violence than others, at length did beat all light from heaven, which like an hell of darkness turned black upon us, so much the more fuller of horror, as in such cases horror and fear use to overrun the troubled and overmastered senses of all, which (taken up with amazement) the ears lay so sensible to the terrible cries and murmurs of the winds and distraction of our company, as who was most armed and best prepared was not a little shaken. For surely . . . as death comes not so sudden nor apparent, so he comes not so elvish and painful (to men especially even then in health and perfect habitudes of body) as at sea; who comes at no time so welcome, but our frailty (so weak is the hold of hope in miserable demonstrations of danger) it makes guilty of many contrary changes and conflicts. For indeed, death is accompanied at no time nor place with circumstances everyway so uncapable of particularities of goodness and inward comforts as at sea.

. . .

For four and twenty hours the storm in a restless tumult had blown so exceedingly as we could not apprehend in our imaginations any possibility of greater violence; yet did we still find it not only more terrible but more constant, fury added to fury, and one storm urging a second more outrageous than the former, whether it so wrought upon our fears, or indeed met with new forces. Sometimes strikes in our ship amongst women and passengers not used to such hurly and discomforts made us look one upon the other with troubled hearts and panting bosoms, our clamours drowned in the winds, and the winds in thunder. Prayers might well be in the heart and lips, but drowned in the outcries of the officers; nothing heard that could give comfort, nothing seen that might encourage hope. . . . [t]he sea swelled above the clouds and gave battle unto heaven. It could not be said to rain; the waters like whole rivers did flood in the air. And this I did still observe, that whereas upon the land, when a storm hath poured itself forth once in drifts of rain, the wind as beaten down and vanquished therewith not long after endureth, here the glut of water, as if throttling the wind erewhile, was no sooner a little emptied and qualified but instantly the winds, as having gotten their mouths now free and at liberty, spake more loud and grew more tumultuous and malignant. What shall I say? Winds and seas were as mad as fury and rage could make them. For mine own part, I had been in some storms before . . . yet all that I had ever suffered gathered together might not hold in comparison with this: there was not a moment in which the sudden splitting or instant oversetting of the ship was not expected.

. . .

Then men might be seen to labour, I may well say, for life, and the better sort, even our governor and admiral themselves, not refusing their turn and to spell each the other, to give example to other . . . testifying how mutually willing they were yet by labour to keep each other from drowning, albeit each one drowned whilst he laboured.

Once so huge a sea broke upon the poop and quarter upon us as it covered our ship from stern to stem like a garment or a vast cloud; it filled her brim-full for a while within, from the hatches up to the spar-deck. . . . [A man] with much clamour encouraged and called upon others, who gave her now up, rent in pieces and absolutely lost. Our governor was at this time below at the capstan, both by his speech and authority heartening every man unto his labour. It struck him from the place where he sat, and grovelled him and all us about him on our faces, beating together with our breaths all thoughts from our bosoms else than that we were now sinking. For my part, I thought her already in the bottom of the sea; and I have heard him say wading out of the flood thereof, all his ambition was but to climb up above hatches to die *in aperto coelo* [in the open air], and in the company of his old friends.

. . .

During all this time the heavens looked so black upon us that it was not possible the elevation of the Pole [star] might be observed, nor a star by night nor sunbeam by day was to be seen. Only upon the Thursday night Sir

George Summers being upon the watch had an apparition of a little round light, like a faint star, trembling and streaming along with a sparkling blaze half the height upon the mainmast, and shooting sometimes from shroud to shroud, tempting to settle as it were upon any of the four shrouds; and for three or four hours together, or rather more, half the night it kept with us, running sometimes along the mainyard to the very end and then returning.

. . .

[W]e much unrigged our ship, threw overboard much luggage, many a trunk and chest (in which I suffered no mean loss) and staved many a butt of beer, hogsheads of oil, cider, wine, and vinegar.

. . .

[I]t being now Friday, the fourth morning, it wanted little but that there had been a general determination to have shut up hatches and, commending our sinful souls to God, committed the ship to the mercy of the sea; surely that night we must have done it, and that night had we then perished. But see the goodness and sweet introduction of better hope by our merciful God given unto us. Sir George Summers, when no man dreamed of such happiness, had discovered and cried land.

[The island]

We found it to be the dangerous and dreaded island, or rather islands, of the Bermuda, whereof let me give your ladyship a brief description before I proceed to my narration. And that the rather, because they be so terrible to all that ever touched on them, and such tempests, thunders, and other fearful objects are seen and heard about them that they may be called commonly the Devil's Islands, and are feared and avoided of all sea travellers alive, above any other place in the world. Yet it pleased our merciful God to make even this hideous and hated place both the place of our safety and means of our deliverance.

And hereby also I hope to deliver the world from a foul and general error, it being counted of most that they can be no habitation for men, but rather given over to devils and wicked spirits; whereas indeed we find them now by experience to be as habitable and commodious as most countries of the same climate and situation, insomuch as if the entrance into them were as easy as the place itself is contenting, it had long ere this been inhabited as well as other islands. Thus shall we make it appear that Truth is the daughter of Time, and that men ought not to deny everything which is not subject to their own sense.

. . .

These islands are often afflicted and rent with tempests, great strokes of thunder, lightning, and rain in the extremity of violence.
. . .

The soil of the whole island is one and the same, the mould dark, red, sandy, dry, and uncapable, I believe, of any of our commodities or fruits. . . . It is like enough that the commodities of the other western islands would prosper there, as vines, lemons, oranges, and sugar canes. . . . There is not through the whole islands either champaign ground [open country], valleys, or fresh rivers. They are full of shaws [thickets] of goodly cedar, fairer than ours here of Virginia, the berries whereof our men seething, straining, and letting stand some three or four days made a kind of pleasant drink.
. . .

Likewise there grow great store of palm trees . . . so broad are the leaves as an Italian umbrella: a man may well defend his whole body under one of them from the greatest storm rain that falls.
. . .

Sure it is that there are no rivers nor running springs of fresh water to be found upon any of them. When we came first we digged and found certain gushings and soft bubblings, which being either in bottoms or on the side of hanging ground were only fed with rain water, which nevertheless soon sinketh into the earth and vanisheth away, or emptieth itself out of sight into the sea, without any channel above or upon the superficies of the earth; for according as their rains fell, we had our wells and pits (which we digged) either half full or absolute exhausted and dry, howbeit some low bottoms (which the continual descent from the hills filled full, and in those flats could have no passage away) we found to continue as fishing ponds or standing pools continually, summer and winter, full of fresh water.

The shore and bays round about when we landed first afforded great store of fish, and that of diverse kinds, and good. . . . We have taken also from under the broken rocks crevises [crayfish] often greater than any of our best English lobsters, and likewise abundance of crabs, oysters, and whelks.
. . .

Fowl there is in great store, small birds, sparrows fat and plump like a bunting, bigger than ours, robins of divers colours, green and yellow, ordinary and familiar in our cabins, and other of less sort. White and grey hernshaws, bitterns, teal, snipes, crows, and hawks, of which in March we found divers aeries, goshawks, and tercels; oxen-birds, cormorants, bald coots, moorhens, owls, and bats in great store. . . . A kind of web-footed fowl there is, of the bigness of an English green plover, or sea-mew [this could be what Shakespeare is referring to when he mentions scamels], which all the summer we saw not, and in the darkest nights of November and December (for in the night they only feed) they would come forth, but not fly far from home, and hovering in the air and over the sea made a strange hollow and harsh howling.

. . .

The tortoise is reasonable toothsome (some say) wholesome meat. I am sure our company liked the meat of them very well, and one tortoise would go further amongst them than three hogs. One turtle (for so we called them) feasted well a dozen messes, appointing six to every mess. It is such a kind of meat as a man can neither absolutely call fish nor flesh.

[Conspiracies and conspirators]

In these dangers and devilish disquiets (whilst the almighty God wrought for us and sent us, miraculously delivered from the calamities of the sea, all blessings upon the shore to content and bind us to gratefulness) thus enraged amongst ourselves to the destruction of each other, into what a mischief and misery had we been given up had we not had a governor with his authority to have suppressed the same? Yet was there a worse practice, faction and conjuration afoot, deadly and bloody, in which the life of our governor, with many others, were threatened, and could not but miscarry in his fall. But such is ever the will of God (who in the execution of his judgments breaketh the firebrands upon the head of him who first kindleth them), there were [those] who conceived that our governor indeed neither durst nor had authority to put in execution or pass the act of justice upon anyone, how treacherous or impious soever; their own opinions so much deceiving them for the unlawfulness of any act which they would execute, daring to justify among themselves that if they should be apprehended before the performance, they should happily suffer as martyrs. They persevered therefore not only to draw unto them such a number and associates as they could work in to the abandoning of our governor and to the inhabiting of this island.

. . .

[E]very man [was] advised to stand upon his guard, his own life not being in safety, whilst his next-neighbour was not to be trusted.

Extract from Sylvester Jourdain, *A Discovery of the Barmudas,* 1610

[The wreck]

All our men, being utterly spent, tired, and disabled for longer labour, were even resolved, without any hope of their lives, to shut up the hatches and to have committed themselves to the mercy of the sea (which is said to be merciless) or rather to the mercy of their mighty God and redeemer. . . . So that some of them, having some good and comfortable waters in the ship, fetched them and drunk the one to the other, taking their last leave one of the other, until their more joyful and happy meeting in a more blessed world; when it pleased God out of his most gracious and merciful providence, so to direct and guide our ship (being left to the mercy of the sea) for her most advantage; that Sir George Somers . . . most wishedly happily descried land.

[The island]

But our delivery was not more strange in falling so opportunely and happily upon the land, as our feeding and preservation was beyond our hopes and all men's expectations most admirable. For the islands of the Bermudas, as every man knoweth that hath heard or read of them, were never inhabited by any Christian or heathen people, but ever esteemed and reputed a most prodigious and enchanted place affording nothing but gusts, storms, and foul weather; which made every navigator and mariner to avoid [them,] as Scylla and Charybdis, or as they would shun the Devil himself; and no man was ever heard to make for the place, but as against their wills, they have by storms and dangerousness of the rocks, lying seven leagues into the sea, suffered shipwreck. Yet did we find there the air so temperate and the country so abundantly fruitful of all fit necessaries for the sustentation and preservation of man's life, that most in a manner of all our provisions of bread, beer, and victual being quite spoiled in lying long drowned in salt water, notwithstanding we were there for the space of nine months (few days over or under) not only well refreshed, comforted, and with good satiety contented but, out of the abundance hereof, provided us some reasonable quantity and proportion of provision to carry us for Virginia. . . . Wherefore my opinion sincerely of this island is, that whereas it hath been and is still accounted the most dangerous, unfortunate, and most forlorn place of the world, it is in truth the richest, healthfulest, and pleasing land (the quantity and bigness thereof considered) and merely natural, as ever man set foot upon.

Extracts from *The True Declaration of the Estate of the Colony in Virginia*, published by the Council of Virginia, 1610

What is there in all this tragical comedy that should discourage us with impossibility of the enterprise? When of all the fleet, one only ship by a secret leak was endangered, and yet in the gulf of despair was so graciously preserved.

[Conspiracies and conspirators in Virginia]

The ground of all those miseries was the permissive providence of God, who, in the forementioned violent storm, separated the head from the body, all the vital powers of regiment being exiled with Sir Thomas Gates in those infortunate (yet fortunate) islands. The broken remainder of those supplies made a greater ship wreck in the continent of Virginia, by the tempest of dissension: every man, overvaluing his own worth, would be a commander; every man, underprizing another's value, denied to be commanded.

New World Utopias

The discovery of societies in the 'new worlds' to the west that operated along very different lines from those of Europe inspired writers such as the French philosopher Michel de Montaigne (1533–92), who speculated about the nature of the indigenous inhabitants of the Americas in his *Essays* (1580). Montaigne saw the social organization of these people as offering lessons to the Europeans and he saw them as exemplifying in some ways an ideal state. In this he was following a long line of writers who had tried to imagine how an ideal state would be organized, including Thomas More in *Utopia* (1516). Shakespeare was clearly interested in questions of state power throughout his career and one of the issues that *The Tempest* dramatizes is how best to organize a state: Prospero had neglected his princely duties in Milan by becoming too interested in magic; his brother and Alonso had operated along Machiavellian lines to displace him. Caliban, Stephano and Trinculo imagine an island ruled by themselves, while Gonzalo imagines an ideal common-wealth in terms that are drawn directly from Montaigne, whose essay title 'Of the Cannibals' itself draws attention to the linguistic prox-imity of the terms 'Caliban', 'Cannibal' and 'Caribbean'.

The main verbal influences on *The Tempest* from Montaigne, in John Florio's 1603 translation, are in Gonzalo's speech beginning at 2.1.145 and in Prospero's thoughts on vengeance beginning at 5.1.27, but, as these extracts indicate, Shakespeare draws on many themes that have parallels in Montaigne.

Extracts from Montaigne's essay 'Of the Cannibals'

[C]ertain Carthaginians having sailed athwart the Atlantic Sea without the Strait of Gibraltar, after a long time they at last discovered a great fertile island replenished with goodly woods and watered with great and deep rivers far distant from all land, and both they and others, allured by the goodness and fertility of the soil, went thither with their wives, chil-dren, and household, and there began to habituate and settle themselves. The lords of Carthage, seeing their country by little and little to be dispeo-pled, made a law and express inhibition that upon pain of death no more men should go thither, and banished all that were gone thither to dwell, fearing (as they said) that in success of time they would so multiply as they might one day supplant them and overthrow their own estate.

. . .

Now (to return to my purpose) I find, as far as I have been informed, there is nothing in that nation that is either barbarous or savage, unless men call that barbarism which is not common to them. As indeed we have no other aim of truth and reason than the example and idea of the opinions and customs of the country we live in. There is ever perfect religion, perfect policy, perfect and complete use of all things. They are even savage as we call those fruits wild which nature of herself and of her ordinary progress hath produced, whereas indeed they are those which ourselves have altered by our artificial devices and diverted from their common order we should rather term savage. In those are the true and most profitable virtues and natural proprieties most lively and vigorous which in these we have bastardized, applying them to the pleasure of our corrupted taste. And if, notwithstanding, in divers fruits of those countries that were never tilled we shall find that in respect of ours they are most excellent and as delicate unto our taste, there is no reason art should gain the point of honour of our great and puissant mother Nature. We have so much by our inventions surcharged the beauties and riches of her works that we have altogether over-choked her; yet wherever her purity shineth, she makes our vain and frivolous enterprises wonderfully ashamed.

. . .

Those nations seem therefore so barbarous unto me because they have received very little fashion from human wit, and are yet near their original naturality. The laws of nature do yet command them, which are but little bastardized by ours. And that with such purity as I am sometimes grieved the knowledge of it came no sooner to light at what time there were men that better than we could have judged of it. I am sorry Lycurgus and Plato had it not, for meseemeth that what in those nations we see by experience doth not only exceed all the pictures wherewith licentious poesy hath proudly embellished the golden age and all her quaint inventions to feign a happy condition of man, but also the conception and desire of philosophy. They could not imagine a genuity [simplicity] so pure and simple as we see it by experience, nor ever believe our society might be maintained with so little art and human combination. It is a nation, would I answer Plato, that hath no kind of traffic, no knowledge of letters, no intelligence of numbers, no name of magistrate nor of politic superiority, no use of service, of riches or of poverty, no contracts, no successions, no dividences [divisions], no occupation but idle, no respect of kindred but common, no apparel but natural, no manuring of lands, no use of wine, corn or metal. The very words that import lying, falsehood, treason, dissimulation, covetousness, envy, detraction, and pardon were never heard of amongst them. How dissonant would he find his imaginary commonwealth from this perfection?

. . .

Furthermore, they live in a country of so exceeding pleasant and temperate situation that, as my testimonies . . . have further assured me, they never saw any man there either shaking with the palsy, toothless, with eyes dropping, or crooked and stooping through age. They are seated alongst the seacoast, encompassed toward the land with huge and sleepy mountains, having between both a hundred leagues or thereabouts of open and champaign ground [open country]. They have great abundance of fish and flesh that have no resemblance at all with ours, and eat them without any sauces or skill of cookery, but plain boiled or broiled. . . . Their drink is made of a certain root, and of the colour of our claret wines, which lasteth but two or three days; they drink it warm. It hath somewhat a sharp taste, wholesome for the stomach, nothing heady, but laxative for such as are not used unto it, yet very pleasing to such as are accustomed unto it.

[Cannibalism]

I am not sorry we note the barbarous horror of such an action, but grieved that prying so narrowly into their faults we are so blinded in ours. I think there is more barbarism in eating men alive than to feed on them being dead; to mangle by tortures and torments a body full of lively sense, to roast him in pieces, to make dogs and swine to gnaw and tear him in mammocks [shreds] (as we have not only read, but seen very lately, yea, and in our own memory, not amongst ancient enemies, but our neighbours and fellow citizens, and – which is worse – under pretence of piety and religion), than to roast and tear him after he is dead.

[. . .] there was never any opinion found so unnatural and immodest that would excuse treason, treachery, disloyalty, tyranny, cruelty, and such like, which are our ordinary faults. We may then well call them barbarous in regard of reason's rules, but not in respect of us that exceed them in all kind of barbarism. Their wars are noble and generous, and have as much excuse and beauty as this human infirmity may admit: they aim at nought so much, and have no other foundation amongst them, but the mere jealousy of virtue. They contend not for the gaining of new lands, for to this day they yet enjoy that natural uberty [abundance] and fruitfulness which without labouring toil doth in such plenteous abundance furnish them with all necessary things that they need not enlarge their limits. They are yet in that happy estate as they desire no more than what their natural necessities direct them; whatsoever is beyond it is to them superfluous. Those that are much about one age do generally enter-call [call each other mutually] one another brethren, and such as are younger they call children, and the aged are esteemed as fathers to all the rest. These leave this full possession of goods in common, and without individuity to their heirs, without other claim or title but that which nature doth plainly impart unto all creatures, even as she brings them into the world.

Extract from Montaigne's essay 'Of Cruelty'

He that through a natural facility and genuine mildness should neglect or contemn injuries received should no doubt perform a rare action, and worthy commendation. But he who, being touched and stung to the quick with any wrong or offence received, should arm himself with reason against this furiously-blind desire of revenge, and in the end, after a great conflict, yield himself master over it, should doubtless do much more. The first should do well, the other virtuously: the one action might be termed goodness, the other virtue.

Prospero's version of this is

> Yet with my nobler reason 'gainst my fury
> Do I take part. The rarer action is
> In virtue than in vengeance. They being penitent,
> The sole drift of my purpose doth extend
> Not a frown further.

(5.i.26–30)

Genre and dramaturgy

The weight of contemporary critical orthodoxy deplored the common dramatic practices of Shakespeare's day as unrealistic and contrary to the received rules of good writing, which were held to have been formulated by the ancient Greek philosopher Aristotle in his *Poetics*. On the basis of his observations of Greek tragedy, Aristotle had suggested that plays worked better if they had one location, took up about 24 hours of imagined stage time and did not have subplots. Although these conventions were not actually observed by many classical Greek plays, the so called 'Unities' of time, place and action were influential in much thinking about writing, so that, for example, the Elizabethan courtier and poet Sir Philip Sidney, writing sometime prior to Shakespeare, had cautioned against many aspects of what would be standard Shakespearean practice, and later critics would use the Unities as sticks to beat Shakespeare with as an untutored ignorant writer. Sidney's posthumously published *Defence of Poesy* (1595, but probably written in the early 1580s since Sidney died in

1586) is an eloquently phrased attack on his contemporaries. Sidney was writing before Shakespeare was active as a dramatist but he scorned plays that used many of the devices that are now familiar to us through Shakespeare's own practice. Favouring the so-called 'Aristotelian Unities' Sidney was particularly scathing on the faults of the dramatists of his period with respect to their failure to observe unity of place and action.

Extracts from Philip Sidney's *Defence of Poesy*, 1595

For where the stage should alway represent but one place, and the utter-most time presupposed in it, should be both by Aristotle's precept, and common reason, but one day; there is both many days and places, inarti-ficially imagined. . . . [Y]ou shall have Asia of the one side, and Africa of the other, and so many other under kingdoms, that the player when he comes in, must ever begin with telling where he is, or else the tale will not be conceived. Now you shall have three ladies walk to gather flowers, and then we must believe the stage to be a garden. By and by we hear news of shipwreck in the same place, then we are to blame if we accept it not for a rock. Upon the back of that, comes out a hideous monster with fire and smoke, and then the miserable beholders are bound to take it for a cave. . . .

Now of time, they [dramatists] are much more liberal. For ordinary it is, that two young princes fall in love, after many traverses she is got with child, delivered of a fair boy: he is lost, groweth a man, falleth in love, and is ready to get another child, and all this in two hours space. Which how absurd it is in sense, even sense may imagine and Art hath taught, and all ancient examples justified. . . . But they will say, how then shall we set forth a story, which contains both many places, and many times? And do they not know that a tragedy is tied to the laws of Poesy and not of History: . . . many things may be told which cannot be showed: if they know the difference betwixt reporting and representing.

Sidney's comments clearly had little impact on the ways in which many dramatists actually wrote for the theatre, and Shakespeare's plays generally fail to comply with Sidney's restrictive prescriptions. In Shakespeare late works *Cymbeline*, *The Winter's Tale* and *Pericles*, epic stories are spread over many years with different devices used to deal with the problems of time passing in precisely the kinds of ways

Sidney objected to. In *The Tempest*, however, Shakespeare appears to be following Sidney's precepts much more closely than he usually did (with the exception of the early *Comedy of Errors*, another play dependent on a shipwreck), using narrative rather than action as a very significant dramatic strategy but also replaying past events through a series of parallels and contrasts. In *The Tempest* Shakespeare seems to have been experimenting with a structure that enabled him to tackle a romance theme within a more neo-classical structure than was usual for him, with very striking results.

Clearly Ben Jonson, who was steeped in neo-classical theory, also found Shakespeare guilty of non-Aristotelian dramaturgy since he specifically alludes to *The Winter's Tale* and *The Tempest* in the Induction to *Bartholomew Fair* (1614), in terms that suggest something of Caliban's contemporary impact: 'If there be never a Servant-monster in the fair, who can help it? . . . [Jonson] is loath to make Nature afraid in his plays, like those that beget Tales, Tempests, and such like Drolleries, to mix his head with other men's heels.' Bartholomew Fair was one of the great London fairs characterized by all kinds of trading, entertainment and exhibitions, and so it represents one of those fairs that Trinculo is alluding to in *The Tempest* when he talks of holiday-fools paying out to see dead Indians (II.ii.28). Jonson offers further incidental testimony of the relevance of America to the Renaissance imagination with the casual remark earlier in the Induction by the Stage-keeper, who is disparaging the author's ability to give a flavour of the true experience of the fair: 'You were even as good go to Virginia for any [atmosphere] there is of Smithfield.'

Anthony Munday's play *John a Kent and John a Cumber* (1594) has a magician aided by a spirit who (invisible to the characters but seen by the audience) plays music and performs very similar tricks to those of Ariel. *A Midsummer Night's Dream* also offers instructive parallels with *The Tempest* in its use of supernatural characters, invisibility as a source of comic confusions and an onstage entertainment for some of the characters. There are also other contemporary parallels with plays such as the anonymous *Mucedorus* (*c.* 1590, but revived in 1610). Shakespeare probably took over *Mucedorus*'s bear for *The Winter's Tale*, while its wild man Bremo, who falls in love with the virginal heroine, has something in common with Caliban.

Tragicomedy, Pastoral and Romance

The Tempest has often been described in terms that locate it within different genres, particularly Tragicomedy, Pastoral, and Romance. Each of these generic categories has something to tell us about how the play works and each shares many elements with the others, so they are best treated together as exemplifying ways of dealing with the nature of the subject matter and how it is treated, particularly the mixture of danger and happy outcomes, the emphasis on wonder and the supernatural, and the emphasis on narrative over characterization.

Philip Sidney disliked the idea of Tragicomedy, in which, as he put it, dramatists were given to 'mingling Kings and Clowns, not because the matter so carrieth it, but thrust in the Clown by head and shoulders to play a part in majestical matters, with neither decency nor discretion'. However, there was a fashion for Tragicomedy in the theatre early in the seventeenth century, deriving from the experimental work of the Italian writer Giovanni Baptista Guarini in the sixteenth century. John Fletcher was a leading exponent of the form, explaining that, as he put it in the preface to his play *The Faithful Shepherdess* (1609–10), 'a tragi-comedy is not so called in respect of mirth and killing, but in respect it wants [i.e. lacks] deaths, which is enough to make it no tragedy, yet brings some near it, which is enough to make it no comedy'. *The Tempest* works well within such a definition, since even the comic plotting of Caliban is aimed at killing Prospero. Although the play is not a conventional Revenge Tragedy, there are very important elements of this genre, particularly characters seeking revenge for being usurped, where the eventual benign outcome is not clear until late in the play.

While *The Tempest* is not obviously a Pastoral, since it does not deal directly with the supposed joys of country living, it does share important elements with the genre of Pastoral, in particular the sense that nature and a wild place offer a necessary corrective to the courtly world and that to be reduced to living in this kind of 'uncivilized' world helps the characters to reassess their value systems. In this sense the island matches such spaces as the Forest of Arden in *As You Like It*, the heath in *King Lear*, or the wood in *A Midsummer Night's*

Dream by offering its inhabitants a chance to participate in a different order of existence and the chance to return to their other world changed by the experience for the better. This links with the utopian ideas expressed by Gonzalo, and many utopian visions assume either the world of the Garden of Eden before Adam and Eve's Fall or the Arcadian Pastoral of the Greek tradition, in which nature is seen as more nurturing of human values than the world of the court and the city.

Pastoral also shares many characteristics with Romance. This term was not used in the Renaissance to refer to such works as *The Tempest*, but it has become quite common to describe Shakespeare's late plays as 'Romances' since the term does point to certain characteristics shared by those plays and the ancient Greek Romances. These early narrative Romances contained a mixture of pastoral episodes and the kind of journeys associated with the epic, while the surprising and the marvellous, and the needs of narrative, took precedence over characterization and plausibility. The most directly relevant of these romances to *The Tempest* is Longus's *Daphnis and Chloe* (*c*. AD 200), both because of some similarities in situations and plots and also because of a number of verbal parallels between the play and Angel Day's 1587 translation of the Greek original. Both works are set on an island, both heroines are virginal, and there is a paternal figure in each who is the only one that can see the character who brings the lovers together (Eros in *Daphnis and Chloe*, Ariel in *The Tempest*). Both contain strange supernatural noises, storms, vanishing banquets, and celebrations involving nymphs and reapers.

Extract from Longus, *Daphnis and Chloe*, translated by Angel Day (1587)

[I]t seemed at night in the midst of their banqueting, that all the land about them was on fire, and a sudden noise arose in their hearing as of a great fleet, and armed navy for the seas, approaching towards them. The sound whereof and dreadful sight, made some of them to cry Arm Arm, and others to gather together their companies, and weapons. One thought his fellow next him was hurt, another feared the shot that he heard rattling in his ears, this man thought his companion slain hard by his side, another seemed to stumble on dead carcasses. In brief, the hurry and tumult was so wonderful and strange, as they almost were at their wits' ends.

This great affray continued in such sort as you have heard all the night long, and that in so terrible manner as that they vehemently wished for the day, hoping in the appearing thereof to be relieved. But yet their rest grew not by the morning's show as was expected, but rather the light thereof discovered unto them far more fearful and strange effects. . . . A dreadful noise was heard from the rocks, not as the sound of any natural trumpets, but far more shrill and hideous.

. . .

[a]bout the midst of the day, the captain of their galleys (not without express divine providence) was cast in a deep and heavy slumber. And as he lay sleeping in his cabin (to the great amaze of all the company, considering those tumults), Pan himself in a vision stood right before him, and . . . he used unto him these or the like speeches following:

'O cruel and mischievous sacrileger, how have you dared with so great and uncontrolled boldness, in arms and show of war, to enter thus cruelly upon my haunts and pastures, dear unto me alone, as whereupon reposeth my special delights? . . . I here protest and denounce unto you, as I am the god Pan . . . that no one of you shall ever see Methimne again . . . but that the sea itself shall soak you up, and your carcasses become a food unto the fishes: Render therefore back again unto the Nymphs their Chloe.'

. . .

The Captain, being awaked of this vision, grew into greater fear and amaze of this heavy charge and speeches.

The court masque

Masques, courtly entertainments of an allegorical kind, often figure in Renaissance plays (Theseus, for example, rejects one before selecting 'Pyramus and Thisbe' in *A Midsummer Night's Dream*), but by the early seventeenth century they had grown in scale and complexity and were attracting major artists such as the architect/designer Inigo Jones and the dramatist Ben Jonson. The entertainment that Prospero lays on for Ferdinand and Miranda in Act IV, scene i, is heavily indebted to these court masques, but the influence of the masque can also be seen elsewhere in the way the play is structured.

Masques were often preceded by antimasques, in which order was disrupted and chaos loomed. In the masques actually performed at court the players in the antimasque were professional actors whereas the players in the masque itself were sometimes courtiers, who would take dance partners from the audience at the culmination of the masque. These masques were themselves in some senses both instruments of government and explorations of what government could and should be. The antimasque was a threat to order, but the restoration of order through courtly dance indicates how statecraft and stagecraft could be equated with one another. Shakespeare's company, the King's Men, were certainly used to performing at court, sometimes in these entertainments. As well as the actual formal entertainment in Act IV, scene i, the strange shapes and Ariel as the harpy in Act III, scene iii, and the hunting with dogs in Act IV, scene i, all suggest an indebtedness to features of the masque and antimasque.

One of Jonson's masques, *Hymenaei*, is particularly relevant to *The Tempest*, not only because of a few verbal and thematic parallels in Jonson's introduction but also because the masque deals with the dangers of lust and the need to control the power of Venus. *Hymenaei* was performed as part of the marriage celebrations of the Earl of Essex to Frances Howard in January 1606. It includes Juno and Iris amongst its cast, and Jonson's description of the setting and costuming (by Inigo Jones) and action gives an idea of the kinds of effects that were possible in the masque. We cannot, of course, simply transfer these details into the staging of the masque in *The Tempest* but they may indicate the kind of effect Shakespeare may have been aspiring to.

Extract from Ben Jonson, *Hymenaei, or the Solemnities of a Masque and Barriers at a Marriage* (1606)

Here, the upper part of the scene, which was all of clouds, and made artificially to swell, and ride like the rack, began to open; and, the air clearing, in the top thereof was discovered Juno, sitting in a throne, supported by two beautiful peacocks; her attire rich, and like a queen, a white diadem on her head, from whence descended a veil, and that bound with a fascia, of several coloured silks, set with all sorts of jewels, and raised in the top with lilies and roses; in her right hand she held a sceptre, in the other a timbrel, at her golden feet the hide of a lion was placed; round about her sat the spirits of the air, in several colours, making music. Above her the region of fire, with a continual motion, was seen to whirl circularly, and Jupiter standing in the top (figuring the heaven) brandishing his thunder: beneath her the rainbow, iris, and, on the two sides eight ladies, attired richly, and alike in the most celestial colours, who represented her powers, as she is the governess of marriage, and made the second masque. All which, upon the discovery, Reason made narration of.

Tunis and Carthage

Recent scholarship has placed a significant emphasis on *The Tempest*'s imaginative indebtedness to the Roman poet Virgil's *Aeneid*, taking its cue from the discussion of 'widow Dido' in Act II, scene i. The *Aeneid* takes up the story of the Trojan hero Aeneas after the fall of Troy, which is the subject of the Greek poet Homer's *Iliad*. The *Aeneid* is modelled on Homer's *Odyssey*, which tells the story of the adventures of the Greek leader Odysseus as he attempts to return home after the Trojan War. Both Aeneas and Odysseus were subject to many adventures in their wanderings about the Mediterranean. In *The Tempest* there are some verbal echoes of Virgil, and Ariel's appearance as a harpy recalls a similar episode in the *Aeneid*. The apparently rather odd debate in Act II, scene i, of the play, about whether Carthage became Tunis, is, as Stephen Orgel has shown, much less odd if one is aware that there were two different traditions about Dido, the Queen of Carthage. In Virgil she is seen as a temptress who delays Aeneas from achieving his destiny of founding Rome, but there was another tradition in which she is seen as a faithful widow. So one function of the debate in the play is to add an element of relativity of perception in a scene that already draws attention to the ways in which the various nobles see the island and their clothes quite differently.

It is difficult to be confident about what connotations Tunis might have had for the Renaissance audience. Certainly Sebastian blames Alonso for loosing (or losing) his daughter to an African, the King of Tunis, but no one specifically mentions that Tunis was a Muslim city. Moreover there had been both English pirates and English naval bases in the city during the period so it would be inappropriate to assume that Shakespeare's audience would have simply equated the town with one or other aspect of either Islam or Africa. What is clear from the context is that Tunis is somewhere outside the norms of European civilization and customs.

Ovid's *Metamorphoses*

One of the few major direct linguistic sources for the play is Medea's speech in the Latin poet Ovid's *Metamorphoses*, which is the basis of Prospero's invocation beginning 'Ye elves of hills, brooks, standing lakes and groves' (V.i.133). Shakespeare appears to have used both the original Latin and the standard Elizabethan translation by Arthur Golding (1567), an extract from which is given here in modernized spelling and punctuation. The speech is spoken by Medea, a witch whose attributes Shakespeare also draws on in characterizing Caliban's mother, Sycorax. Although Prospero's speech is justly famous for the quality of its verse and is rhetorically appropriate to its context, there is no evidence elsewhere in the play that it is an accurate description of Prospero's powers.

> Ye charms and witchcrafts, and thou earth, which both with herb and
> weed
> Of mighty working furnishest the wizards at their need;
> Ye airs and winds; ye elves of hills, of brooks, of woods alone,
> Of standing lakes, and of the night, approach ye every one,
> Through help of whom (the crooked banks much wond'ring at the thing)
> I have compelled streams to run clean backward to their spring.
> By charms I make the calm seas rough, and make the rough seas plain,
> And cover all the sky with clouds and chase them thence again.
> By charms I raise and lay the winds and burst the viper's jaw,
> And from the bowels of the earth both stones and trees do draw.
> Whole woods and forests I remove; I make the mountains shake,
> And even the earth itself to groan and fearfully to quake.
> I call up dead men from their graves; and thee, O lightsome Moon,
> I darken oft, though beaten brass abate thy peril soon;
> Our sorcery dims the morning fair, and darks the sun at noon.

Prospero's version of this is as follows:

> Ye elves of hills, brooks, standing lakes, and groves,
> And ye that on the sands with printless foot
> Do chase the ebbing Neptune, and do fly him
> When he comes back; you demi-puppets that
> By moonshine do the green sour ringlets make,
> Whereof the ewe not bites; and you whose pastime
> Is to make midnight mushrooms, that rejoice
> To hear the solemn curfew, by whose aid –
> Weak masters though ye be – I have bedimmed
> The noontide sun, called forth the mutinous winds,
> And 'twixt the green sea and the azured vault
> Set roaring war; to the dread rattling thunder
> Have I given fire, and rifted Jove's stout oak
> With his own bolt; the strong-based promontory
> Have I made shake, and by the spurs plucked up
> The pine and cedar; graves at my command
> Have waked their sleepers, oped and let 'em forth
> By my so potent art.
>
> (V.i.135–50)

Savage men

Contemporary debates about the importance of nature and nurture in determining how people behaved drew heavily on the encounters between Europeans and Americans, with some Europeans (like Montaigne) emphasizing the natural innocence of the Americans and others seeing them as lacking in the civilized qualities instilled by a Christian upbringing. One of the great paradoxes in such attitudes to nature was that it was seen as at once purer and less corrupted than civilization, and at the same time as in need of taming, training, and education. In *The Tempest* Shakespeare contrasts Caliban, an apparently uneducable savage, with Antonio and Sebastian, who, though educated, behave equally savagely towards their companions. Shakespeare was not only influenced by interest in the indigenous inhabitants of the New World but also drew on a long-established European tradition, that of the wild man of the woods, often called 'wodewose'. In the Folio cast list Caliban is described as 'a salvage and deformed slave'. Some critics attach no significance to the spelling 'salvage', regarding it as simply meaning 'savage'; others suggest that the spelling points us towards the word's original connotations of the countryside. In either case, Caliban does manifest many of the characteristics of these feral men as depicted in both literature and art, including Bremo in the anonymous *Mucedorus*, which was revived by the King's Men just before the staging of *The Tempest*. Sometimes these wild men displayed signs of innate goodness, turning out to be long-lost scions of the aristocracy; sometimes, like Bremo, they were ogreish figures with bestial characteristics.

Magic and alchemy

The alchemist John Dee (1527–1608), who is sometimes seen as a 'source' for Prospero, provides a good case study of the various intersections between astronomy, alchemy, astrology, science, philosophy and the state. Although to modern eyes his more scientific interests (mathematics, astronomy and navigation) clash with alchemy and astrology, Dee saw his activities as part of a sustained attempt to master the underlying forces of nature and they brought him into contact with the court for over fifty years. He got into serious trouble for casting the horoscopes of Queen Mary and the then Princess Elizabeth and when Elizabeth became queen he advised her on a range of issues ranging from astrology to navigation. His efforts to enhance his understanding led him to try to contact angels for help and he enlisted the help of one Edward Kelley as his go-between. One of Kelley's supposed supernatural contacts was an angel with the resonant name Uriel. Kelley and Dee spent much time in Europe, where Dee met the Holy Roman Emperor and the King of Poland before returning to England where he found that his home and his cherished library had been robbed and vandalized by people who thought that he was involved in black magic. Elizabeth then made him warden of a college in Manchester but this was not a great success, and when the fiercely anti-magic James VI of Scotland became James I of England in 1603, Dee was left to his own devices.

Dee's career may have influenced three of the great Renaissance plays that deal with magic. Christopher Marlowe's *Doctor Faustus* (1588) derives from the Faust legend but was written at a time when Dee was an increasingly controversial figure. Dee's reputation as an alchemist may have contributed to Ben Jonson's presentation of a con-man alchemist in *The Alchemist*, staged by the King's Men in 1610. The same actor, Richard Burbage, probably played both Subtle the alchemist in Jonson's play and Prospero in Shakespeare's.

Contemporary attitudes to magic were highly complex and, although much scholarly energy has been devoted to establishing the exact nature of Prospero's magic status, we cannot be sure how great a percentage of a contemporary audience would have been able to differentiate between the various elements in his presentation. At one level Prospero's magic is contrasted with that of Sycorax, Caliban's mother: he insists that she was a witch who was in league with evil, whereas he is a good person whose energies are devoted to trying to understand the mysteries of the universe. Yet it is he who appropriates Medea's speech from Ovid in Act 5, scene i, and recently Jonathan Bate has made a convincing case that at least some of Shakespeare's audience would have been familiar enough with the uses of that speech elsewhere for it to problematize any tendency to see him as a white magician or magus. Certainly Prospero's claim to have waked the dead is not unproblematic, if one believes it, since he actually does nothing like it in the play.

Even Prospero's need for wood may have reminded some of the audience of one of the perennial problems of the alchemist's search for the Philosopher's Stone, which was to keep a fire going for a long time at a constant heat. For example, the unlucky and obscure alchemist Thomas Charnock was constantly preoccupied with this problem (Hughes, 40–6). Prospero uses terms that had alchemical connotations and this may have reminded some of the audience of the fraudulent schemes of tricksters like Subtle, particularly if both parts were played by the same actor, and even the play's title can refer to a significant moment in the alchemical process.

Like Faustus, Prospero spends years in study before he can contact the spirit world, but unlike Faustus he does not cross over the line that divides scientific inquiry from black magic. One of the ironies of

Faustus's pact with evil is that he ends up performing magic that equates very readily with the sleight of hand of professional conjurers. There is also an ironic level to the presentation of Prospero's magic arts, which at some levels are virtuoso examples of stage trickery (the device to hide the banquet in the harpy scene probably involves a trick table top of a kind still used by stage magicians today): Prospero's mastery of magic spectacle also demonstrates Shakespeare's technical mastery of theatrical effect.

Analogies between magic and political government were not lost on Renaissance society: James I had written both on the problems of magic, when he was James VI of Scotland (*Demonology*, 1597), and on government (in the form of advice to his son Henry on how to be a good king, in *Basilicon Doron*, 1598). Although contemporary sceptics such as Reginald Scot spent considerable effort on debunking popular beliefs in witchcraft and magic (in *A Discovery of Witchcraft*, 1584), even explaining the mechanisms of tricks, such sceptics were in a minority and James was concerned enough about Scot's potentially dangerous influence to order the destruction of his book when he became King of England in 1603.

Government in state and family

In *The Tempest* the question of government is linked to ideas about the ideal commonwealth, since, as Antonio accurately but unkindly points out, Gonzalo's prescription for his utopian world involves the paradox that creating a more 'natural' society requires a high degree of governmental intervention. A perennial issue for any state is the relationship between the rulers and the ruled, the implied contract which allows for a society to develop structures that regulate human interaction by both implicit and explicit codes of sanctioned and forbidden behaviour. One of the key questions is by what right a person can exercise power and what rights other people may have to terminate that power. *The Tempest* is in many ways a dramatic laboratory in which various hypotheses about government can be tested: Caliban claims he should rule the island because he was born there and should succeed his mother, who was the first inhabitant;

Prospero's claim to govern Caliban is based on his superior nature and education and the argument that Caliban proved his unfitness to rule when he attempted to rape Miranda; Prospero neglected his duties as ruler of Milan by getting too engrossed in his studies; Sebastian and Antonio's attempt to kill Alonso is based on nothing more than the will to wield power, while Stephano is attracted by the trappings of power and the possibility of sex with Miranda. All of these viewpoints raise important issues. Family relationships were held to be analogous with those between rulers and the ruled, as this extract from James VI's *Basilicon Doron* suggests:

> For the part of making, and executing of Laws, consider first the true difference betwixt a lawful good King, and an usurping Tyrant. . . . The one acknowledgeth himself ordained for his people, having received from God a burden of government, whereof he must be countable: The other thinketh his people ordained for him, a prey to his passions and inordinate appetites, as the fruits of his magnanimity: And therefore, as their ends are directly contrary, so are their whole actions, as means, whereby they press to attain to their ends. A good King, thinking his highest honour to consist in the due discharge of his calling, employeth all his study and pains, to procure and maintain, by the making and execution of good Laws, the welfare and peace of his people; and as their natural father and kindly Master, thinketh his greatest contentment standeth in their prosperity, and his greatest surety in having their hearts, subjecting his own private affections and appetites to the weal and standing of his Subjects, ever thinking common interest his chiefest particular: whereby the contrary, an usurping Tyrant, thinking his greatest honour and felicity to consist in attaining . . . to his ambitious pretences, thinketh never himself sure, but by the dissension and factions among his people, and counterfeiting the Saint while he once creep in credit, will then (by inverting all good Laws to serve only for his unruly private affections) frame the commonweal ever to advance his particular: building his surety upon his people's misery: and in the end (as a stepfather and an uncouth hireling) make up his own hand upon the ruins of the Republic.

Marriage was a recognized way of cementing political alliances in courtly circles (*The Tempest* was played at court as part of the celebrations of one such political alliance, the marriage of James's daughter to the Elector Palatine) and clearly Ferdinand and Miranda's marriage offers a way of reconciling the clashing political interests of Prospero and Alonso. Presumably something similar underlies Alonso's decision to marry Claribel to the King of Tunis. Although the play itself is largely silent on the reasons for that marriage, Sebastian makes some trenchant points about Claribel's unhappiness at the proposed marriage: 'the fair soul herself / Weighed between loathness and obedience at / Which end o'th'beam should bow' (II.i.131–3). As this suggests, families were regarded as microcosms of the state, with power invested in the father, and children bound to operate under the control of their parents. Both Ferdinand and Miranda are aware of the power of the father, which in Ferdinand's case extends to his right to succeed his supposedly drowned father as King of Naples. Ferdinand is very concerned about due process: he knows that for dynastic reasons it is important that he marries a virgin, and he apologizes to Alonso for taking a decision to marry without his permission, justifying this by his belief that his father is dead. Miranda is a more interesting case since she challenges her father's power on at least two occasions. When she intervenes to try to stop Prospero ill-treating Ferdinand in Act I, scene ii, Prospero's response ('What, I say, / My foot my tutor?', ll. 469–70) draws on the idea of the body as a microcosm of social order. In Act III, scene i, Miranda tells Ferdinand her name and immediately reacts guiltily ('O my father, / I have broke your hest to say so!' ll. 36–7) before proceeding to accept the marriage proposal without reference to her father. Although the sense of rebellion is mitigated by our knowledge that all this is sanctioned by Prospero, who is actually watching them, convention demanded that children were guided by their parents in the choice of marriage partners, as this extract from John Dod and Robert Cleaver's *A Godly Form of Household Government* (1598) demonstrates:

> young folks ought not to be too rash and hasty in their choice, but to have the good advice and direction of their parents and trusty friends in this behalf, who have better judgment, and are more free from the motions of all affections, than they are. And they must take heed, lest following the light and corrupt judgment of their own affections and minds, they change not a short delectation and pleasure, into a continual sorrow and repentance. For we do learn, by great and continual use and experience of things, that the secret contracts made between those that be young do

seldom prosper, whereas contrariwise, those marriages that are made and
established by the advice of wise and religious parents, do prosper well.

Service and slavery

The stress on different approaches to power, who should exercise it
and why, is one of the reasons why *The Tempest* is so open to readings
that stress the question of power in relation to colonialism and to
slavery. Slavery was not, of course, simply a matter of white exploita-
tion of Africans since there were many white slaves (particularly relevant here may be those English citizens who were enslaved in galleys
operating out of ports such as Tunis), and many black Africans were
willing actors in enslaving members of other tribes. However, one of
the contrasts in *The Tempest* is between Caliban, the slave, and Ariel,
who has a contractual relationship which allows him to be freed at
the end of a term of service. Such forms of agreement between
masters and labourers were used routinely in both England and the
new colonies but even if they were often heavily weighted against the
indentured servant, they were based on mutual obligations. Caliban,
on the other hand, has no hope of release from his bondage, which
has been imposed on him as a punishment for attempting to rape
Miranda. This justification of Caliban's enslavement parallels similar
explanations of the subordination of native peoples that occurs in
many European narratives of relationships between indigenous
peoples and the colonizers, including those rehearsed in the
accounts of the relationship between the settlers in Virginia and the
Powhatan tribe, to which Pocahontas belonged.

Names

Shakespeare was eclectic in the sources he used for names in *The
Tempest* and there are sometimes a range of possibilities he might
have drawn from. However, Caliban, a near anagram of both cannibal and Carib, probably derives from Shakespeare's reading of
Montaigne; Setebos, the god worshipped by Caliban's mother

Sycorax, probably comes from Robert Eden's *History of Travel* (1577); some of the Italian names come from William Thomas's *History of Italy* (1549) but Prospero and Stephano are also characters' names in Jonson's first version of *Every Man in His Humour* (1598), a play that Shakespeare himself had acted in. Miranda, as the play makes clear, means 'wonder'; and Shakespeare used the name Antonio on several occasions, notably in *The Merchant of Venice* and *Twelfth Night*.

Other analogues and influences

The sheer diversity of the works that have been proposed as sharing some similarities with *The Tempest* is proof that Shakespeare was drawing on what Geoffrey Bullough calls 'a large international body of folklore and romantic tradition' (p. 249). He made that comment in dismissing the claims of Jacob Ayrer's *Die Schöne Sidea*, translated into English in 1618, to have been a source for Shakespeare's play. Ayrer has an exiled magician-duke whose daughter falls in love with his enemy's son, who is then forced to carry logs, but similar elements are also to be found in some extant *Commedia dell' arte* scenarios. There is no proof that Shakespeare knew these specific scenarios, nor any provable connection between his work and Ayrer's, so they remain useful examples to demonstrate how available these kinds of motifs were to writers of the period, rather than proofs of direct influence.

4 Key Productions and Performances

The Tempest was supplanted for many years, in the theatre, by an adaptation which only gave way to a more or less Shakespearean version during the first half of the nineteenth century. It was effectively replaced by versions derived ultimately from an adaptation by John Dryden and William Davenant, first performed in 1667, that held the stage for some 170 years in the face of occasional more Shakespearean versions. The Dryden/Davenant *Tempest* usually gets a bad critical press as a sacrilegious assault on Shakespeare, but, as its 1959 professional revival, as part of the Purcell celebrations, showed, it works well in its own right, and recent academic interest has also helped to rescue it from the charge of mindless mangling. Dryden and Davenant addressed one problematic aspect of the original *Tempest* as a comedy, creating a traditional cross-purposes romantic plot between a quartet of would-be lovers by providing Miranda with a sister Dorinda and introducing Hippolito (a breeches part), who has never seen a woman, to parallel Miranda. In 1674 the Dryden/Davenant *Tempest* was further altered by Thomas Shadwell, with more songs, music and dancing (and burlesqued by Thomas Duffett as *The Mock Tempest, or The Enchanted Castle*, in which Miranda and Dorinda work as prostitutes). This adaptation became the basis for most productions until 1838, with actor-managers such as David Garrick or John Philip Kemble putting in more or less Shakespeare and adding or removing songs as their artistic and commercial instincts dictated. The adaptation acquired distinguished music by Henry Purcell, Thomas Arne and Thomas Linley along the way but gradually lost its original vitality as changes multiplied over the decades.

By 1838, when William Charles Macready replaced the Dryden/
Davenant-inspired version with a production that was more wholly
Shakespearean (though, given the habits of Victorian managers,
somewhat truncated for reasons of decorum and to accommodate
realistic scenery, spectacular effects and music), there was no independent tradition of staging Shakespeare's play. Macready's approach
was cautiously spectacular, thus paving the way for a whole series of
highly elaborate productions in which the Shakespearean text was in
competition with scenery and music designed to enhance the audience's sensory pleasure, but increasingly at the cost of subtlety of
interpretation. Macready's storm scene was highly spectacular and
managed without Shakespeare's dialogue:

> A tranquil sea – the Neapolitan fleet in the distance – a storm suddenly
> rises – thunder and lightning – the fleet is dispersed – dark clouds descend
> and obscure the vessels – demons appear above, waving intermitting
> lights – a shattered vessel appears R. – is dismasted – founders – Ariel
> passes over the stage waving an intermitting light – grand panoramic
> spectacle. (*The Tempest*, London: J. Pattie, 1839)

Such grand spectacles were to become the key element in subsequent productions. Macready established a norm for the nineteenth
century in which the play's apparent lack of dramatic conflict was
shored up by music and spectacular scenery, which in turn meant
that large amounts of text were jettisoned to make room for them,
thus further exacerbating the supposed failings of the play. For
example, Charles Kean's 1857 *Tempest* depended on a spectacular staging that outstripped anything that had preceded it. According to the
playbills, 'the kind indulgence of the public is requested should any
lengthened delay take place between the acts'. The storm was played
as 'an introduction to the Play', after which the curtain descended and
the overture was played 'for the purpose of giving time for the clearing away and re-setting of the Stage'. Stage mechanics clearly took
precedence over continuity of action. On the first night, difficulties
with the machinery, which had already delayed the opening, resulted
in over five and a half hours in the theatre. Hans Christian Andersen
commented:

On the first night we were there from seven o'clock until twelve-thirty in the morning. Everything was afforded that machinery and stage direction can provide, and yet after seeing it, one felt overwhelmed, tired and empty. Shakespeare was lost in visual pleasure; the exciting poetry was petrified by illustrations; the living world had evaporated. No one tasted the spiritual banquet – it was forgotten for the golden platter on which it was served.   (Marker, pp. 20–3)

The rediscovery in 1888 of the so-called De Wit drawing of the Swan theatre, new scholarly work and William Poel's attempts to stage 'authentic' Renaissance productions led to a growing under-standing in the 1890s of the realities of production in the Renaissance period and, coupled with financial pressures on managers, eventually led to a greater simplicity in staging Shakespeare (see Styan, and O'Connor). By 1904, when Herbert Beerbohm Tree offered a staging that became a byword for the over-spectacular, thoughtful critics were condemning the tradition of 'upholstering' Shakespeare. The *Daily Chronicle*, for example, argued that Tree's realistic shipwreck 'failed to prove even so appealing as the device resorted to a year or two back by members of the Elizabethan Stage Society. They . . . allowed their mariners to pretend to be wrecked in a simple balcony above the stage – with a result that was curiously effective' (15 September 1904). This was a reference to Poel's 1897 production, which had appealed, naturally enough, to the iconoclastic Bernard Shaw: 'where a stage ship would be absurd, the use of the singing gallery makes no attempt to impose on us: it disarms criticism by unaffected submission to the facts of the case, and throws itself honestly on our fancy with instant success' (Shaw, p. 242). Some crit-ics clearly felt that Tree had gone overboard and he was moved to defend himself (as Kean also had), declaring that of all Shakespeare's plays, *The Tempest* was the one that 'most demands the aid of modern stagecraft' (Tree's programme note). One of the aids of modern stage-craft available to Tree was the cinema and he made a two-minute film of his storm scene. The American distributor describes it thus:

The lightnings flash, the billows leap and roll and break until on the toss-ing ship where the terror stricken voyagers can be seen wildly rushing about, the mast snaps and crashes to the deck. Three views are given in the film, each from a more distant point as the wreck recedes and as the film is issued tinted to the suitable weird moonlight colour, the effect obtained is very fine.

Unfortunately the film is now lost, but many subsequent directors would turn to film as a means of tackling some of the staging challenges of *The Tempest*.

The restoration of Shakespeare's text as the normal stage version in the nineteenth century had the effect of dehumanizing the stage Prospero, who had been a harassed father, mage and would-be ruler in the adaptations, and turning him into an unproblematically patriarchal figure. In 1838 the poet Thomas Campbell suggested a link between Prospero and Shakespeare, so it became possible to see the play as representing not just Prospero's but also Shakespeare's farewell to his art. No one in the nineteenth-century theatre appears to have considered that the father of a teenager need not be more than in his mid-thirties, rather than the grandfather his physical embodiment often suggested. The view that *The Tempest* was Shakespeare's last play before he retired contributed to the development of a picture of an aged writer returning to Stratford and a life of contemplation that actually contradicted both the facts known about Shakespeare at the time and the play itself, where Prospero intends to return to Milan as its ruler, having secured a dynastic marriage that will ensure his family's increased power in Italy. Nineteenth-century Prosperos were, therefore, generally calm, saintly, benign and old, emphasizing the decorative and static rather than the active and dynamic. Actor-managers were used to playing the major roles in the plays they produced but Charles Kean, who staged a very spectacular *Tempest* in 1857, could find no suitable part for himself, and subsequently Frank Benson and Beerbohm Tree both chose to play Caliban rather than Prospero, presumably because, although the part is much shorter, it seemed to offer more opportunities to the actor. In the Dryden/Davenant version Caliban is mainly a comic wild man and a channel for anti-democratic attitudes but throughout the nineteenth century Shakespeare's Caliban came to be seen as representing variously the oppressed proletariat, downtrodden indigenous peoples and a Darwinian missing link between humanity and the apes.

In 1848, a year of great political turmoil throughout Europe, William and Robert Brough staged a burlesque, *The Enchanted Isle*, in which Caliban was identified with anti-slavery campaigns and revolutionary activity, entering to the strains of the Marseillaise wearing a 'Cap of Liberty' and carrying a red flag (Booth, p. 186). Daniel Wilson's book *Caliban: The Missing Link* (1870) suggested that Shakespeare had anticipated the idea of a missing link in the Darwinian evolutionary chain, an idea that certainly seems to have influenced Frank Benson in his 1890s production. According to his less than enchanted wife Constance, he spent hours in the zoo observing monkeys and baboons to inform an interpretation in which, wearing a costume all too accurately described as 'half-monkey, half-coconut' he would hang head down from property trees and carry a real fish in his mouth (Constance Benson, p. 179; Trewin, p. 150). Benson tried to bring out Caliban's responsiveness to the music of the island and to capitalize on a strand of liberal opinion that had begun to develop ideas that used Caliban to represent the victims of both capitalism and colonialism, but Tree went further by addressing an issue that Shakespeare had not addressed at all: the ultimate fate of Caliban. The play is silent on whether Caliban leaves or not, but Tree ended his very spectacular production with a tableau of Caliban stretching out his arms towards the departing ship 'in mute despair', deserted 'on the lonely rock' but 'a king once more' (*Tempest*, 1904, p. 63). Tree's reading was clear to his audience, if controversial: Caliban was a representative of the colonized who learnt too late that he needed the wise rule of the colonizer. On the other hand, Ivor Brown in the *Observer* began to review successive Calibans in terms of his belief that he should be as much 'a case for the radical politician's sympathy as for Prospero's punishment' (*Observer*, 14 January 1934) (see Griffiths for more details). However, in Britain, it was not until 1970 that Jonathan Miller offered a production in which anti-colonialism became a central element.

In the interim, at the age of 26, John Gielgud had embarked on a series of Prosperos spaced over 60 years that would culminate in his appearance in *Prospero's Books*. Gielgud first played the part in 1930 (directed by Harcourt Williams), and then again in 1940 (George Devine and Marius Goring), 1957 (Peter Brook) and 1974 (Peter Hall).

Although his successive performances differed in some respects, he made a point of never looking at his Ariels (Gielgud, *Shakespeare*, p. 111). Gielgud played a major part in banishing the old stage tradition, which was aptly summed up by Ivor Brown in 1930: 'Tradition has . . . insisted that Prospero would be an eminent Victorian in a dressing-gown, equipped with a beard beyond the dreams of Marx–Ibsen and W. G. Grace, faintly episcopal in manner, and profoundly tedious in effect.' However, Gielgud's Prospero, clean shaven, according to Gielgud (p. 109), on the basis of a suggestion from the director Theodore Komisarjevsky, was 'an Italian noble . . . the world weary exile . . . no longer a patriarch spilling his words into his whiskers, but a middle-aged man who delivers his poetry as if it meant something' (Brown, *Manchester Guardian*, 8 October 1930). Even in 1940 *The Times* appeared almost surprised to discover 'nothing in the text of The Tempest to conflict with Mr. John Gielgud's idea of the master spirit of the enchanted island as a scholarly Italian nobleman of middle age, lightly bearded and, though accustomed to reading spectacles, well preserved'. By 1957, Gielgud, who was playing the part as being about his own actual age, was beardless again 'with the grizzled hair of virile middle-age and half bared to the waist' (*The Times*, 14 August); by 1974, when he was seventy, he was made up to resemble John Dee, the Renaissance mage (Gielgud, *Actor*, p. 204).

Although Gielgud's physical appearance in the early productions did much to dispel Prospero's patriarchal image, the most important element of his approach was that he discovered a conflict in Prospero that enabled him to break out of the conventional image of serene control and find a character who was much more interesting than the bland traditional patriarch. Gielgud noted that: 'Prospero is really very difficult; he is a very passionate man, but he doesn't have any real contact with the other characters, and he can easily become either priggish, or boring, or didactic. There is not a single grain of humour in him,' and in 1957 he tried to 'play it with strength and passion, as a kind of Jacobean revenge drama. The whole action of the play is Prospero growing to the final understanding that hatred and revenge are useless' (Morley, pp. 375, 283). There is a hint of this as early as the 1930 staging when Gielgud's great-uncle Fred Terry wrote to his grandmother Kate Terry, wondering if Gielgud was 'right to be as "angry" with Ariel as he is with "the monster"?' (quoted in Hayman, p. 68) . In finding Prospero's anger with Ariel, we can see that Gielgud was anticipating an element that would become of major importance much later in the century.

The productions Gielgud played in encapsulated many ways of approaching Prospero: in 1930 Prospero was a world-weary conjuror in a vaguely oriental fantasy setting; in 1940 his directors wanted 'a vigorous Prospero still at the height of his powers and full of passion for life' (Hayman, p. 128); in Brook's 1957 production, Gielgud continued to demonstrate that he had found a way of reducing the part's problems by stressing an inner psychological conflict to be found in the words, and the ending was conceived as his victory; in 1974 Peter Hall wanted Gielgud to play Prospero 'as a disillusioned man who had kept his old court suit in his cave for twenty years and got it out very reluctantly. He felt that Prospero did not want his dukedom back and resented having to leave his island' (Gielgud, *Actor*, p. 202). In Hall's masque-influenced production, according to Irving Wardle, Caliban wore a bisected make-up, 'one half the ugly scrofulous monster whom Prospero sees, on the other an image of the noble savage . . . striving to break from the first stage into the second' (*The Times*, 6 March 1974). This ingenious way of visualizing two key elements of the ways Caliban was regarded paid no attention to another strand which was again becoming important, the idea that the play said something about the colonial experience.

Aimé Césaire's *Une Tempête* (1969) was partly a response to Octave Mannoni's *Prospero and Caliban: The Psychology of Colonialism* (see Chapter 6 'Critical Assessments'), which explicitly reimagined the contest between Prospero and Caliban as one between the exploitative colonizer and the indigenous population. In England, Jonathan Miller's 1970 production put the issue firmly back on the agenda. Itself inspired by Mannoni's writings, Miller's production was the most overtly colonial one in Britain since Tree's, although its analysis was very far removed from its remote predecessor's. Ariel and Caliban (played by the black actors Norman Beaton and Rudolph Walker) embodied two ways in which indigenous populations reacted to their colonizers: Ariel copied European ways and he picked up Prospero's broken wand in order to exert power over Caliban, whom Miller described as 'a detribalized field hand, with faint memories of matrilineal gods' (see Griffiths). Miller's reading extended the colonial dimension from the Prospero–Caliban relationship to the Prospero–Ariel relationship and, following the hint of Gielgud's 1930 interpretation, stressed the importance of the power that Prospero exerts over Ariel to keep him under control.

Giorgio Strehler's Italian-language version of *The Tempest* for Milan's Piccolo theatre (originally 1978) was very influential throughout Europe with its stress on the play's engagement with issues of theatricality. The mechanics of the magic effects were clearly visible as Strehler attempted to make metatheatrical points about the possibilities and limitations of art. Something similar happened in the Japanese Ninagawa Company's version seen in Britain in 1988 and 1992. The production's concept was that a contemporary director is staging a Noh version of *The Tempest* on the island of Sado where Zeami, founder of the Noh theatre, was banished in the fifteenth century. There was a very strong emphasis on theatricality and on the theme of exile in this production, which carried forward into many later British stagings.

Although Philip Osment's *This Island's Mine* (1988) deals with an attempt to stage *The Tempest* in which a black actor is at the mercy of his white director's demands that he play Caliban to fit more closely with the director's own ideas about authentic black experience, increasingly the Prospero–Ariel relationship would be seen as a key element in production and the moment of his release was often crucial to these interpretations. Sam Mendes's 1993 RSC revival was noteworthy for stressing the relationship between Prospero and Ariel (played by Alec McCowen and Simon Russell Beale). Michael Billington thought there were dangers in an approach that treated the play as 'a meta-theatrical spectacle' since 'the colonialist politics' could be lost and Prospero could become 'an omnipotent puppet-master'. However, in this case, Mendes was able to remind the audience that Prospero is, in some ways, as much a usurper as his brother. While Caliban cowers before Miranda and treats his master's language with care,

> Prospero never lets Ariel forget who is boss . . . this pays off sensationally
> in the final moments when the delicate spirit, finally given his freedom,
> unequivocally spits in his master's face.   (*Guardian*, 13 August 1993)

This moment marks a high point in the transfer of the fulcrum
of colonial interpretations from the interaction between Prospero
and Caliban to that between Prospero and Ariel. While female
Ariels have often had a quasi-erotic relationship with Prospero,
thus leaving Caliban as the clearly recalcitrant servant, Ariels had
also been becoming more antagonistic, but Ariel's gesture was a
major innovation. It proved highly controversial. John Peter
thought it was 'a disastrous slip', claiming that Prospero was a
magician who created wonderful theatre, a 'playwright within the
play', but that he was also ruling a magical island, commanding a
creative spirit in the person of Ariel, and a destructive one, Caliban.
The Tempest was, among other things, political dealing with questions of moral and social order. According to Peters, Marx might
well have disagreed with Shakespeare's conclusion in which the
obedient were freed and the rebellious crushed, but Stephano and
Trinculo would have represented one of his political *bêtes noire*, the
useless *lumpenproletariat*:

> We ourselves may not go for the notion of benevolent colonialism
> which is implicit in the play; but at the same time Shakespeare raises
> questions about the nature of rule and submission, command and
> obedience, revolt and compromise, which would have engaged modern
> thinkers as diverse as Marx, Franz Fanon or Michel Foucault.   (*Sunday
> Times*, August 15)

By the time the production reached the Barbican the spitting had
been cut. However, it remains an important example of the ways in
which interpretations of the play were developing and, although it
takes Ariel's unhappiness to an extreme, it is not gratuitous, since the
play offers ample evidence that the Prospero–Ariel relationship is
less than harmonious. Patrick Stewart's Prospero in George C.
Wolfe's 1995 New York adaptation developed this point in a performance that combined Gielgud's idea of inner turmoil with a complex
relationship with Ariel. Stewart was

a quirky, nuanced magician who could convince us that he had to struggle with revenge even after deciding intellectually that 'not a hair' of his
enemies would perish and even after prompting the love-at-first-sight of
Miranda and Ferdinand . . . Prospero's passion had to find compassion.
. . . Prospero had paused for a long time, his staff threatening to descend
upon a cringing Ariel, who had dared to say 'Mine would, sir, were I
human.' The frozen image asked, literally, whether Prospero would crush
his own spirit – Ariel and his own soul. That Ariel was played by a young
and beautiful woman (Aunjanue Ellis) made the situation even more
threatening than it was merely by dint of Prospero's poised staff. Stewart
very quietly said, 'And mine shall.'   (Coursen)

Where Dryden and Davenant had literally expanded Prospero's
family, late twentieth-century interpretations recognized familial
dynamics in Shakespeare's own characters. When Adrian Noble
directed the play for the Royal Shakespeare Company in 1998 he
thought that Prospero had 'made Caliban into a dependent child who
becomes an outcast and so does Ariel; when he asks a question about
being given his freedom all hell comes down on him. I always feel
that Prospero has brought all the patterns of a dysfunctional family
to the island' (*Birmingham Post*, 7 February 1998). A new trend in interpretations of the role by female Ariels meant that the old linking of
Caliban and Ariel as servants was joined by new ones as Ariel and
Miranda sometimes became quasi-sisters. Sometimes the relationship between Prospero and Ariel took on a potentially erotic dimension; sometimes connections between patriarchy and imperialism
were further explored in the Prospero–Miranda relationship.

Female Prosperos such as Vanessa Redgrave gave an added impetus to this part of the equation. At Shakespeare's Globe in 2000 her
Prospero was 'a younger Mother Courage' according to Sheridan
Morley (*Spectator*, 3 June). Despite Redgrave's long-standing association with the Workers' Revolutionary Party, Nicholas de Jongh
thought that she was harking back 'to Victorian notions of Prospero
as the noble colonial ruler', ignoring 'modern belief that the Tempest
was Shakespeare's critique of Elizabethan and Jacobean empire-
building. And since this actress prefers to play sufferers, saviours and
saints, she suppresses signs of Prospero's tyrannical tendencies and
desire for vengeance' (*Evening Standard*, 30 May). Jasper Britton as

Caliban harked back to the days of F. R. Benson: he was, according to Georgina Brown, 'an ugly, stinking beast of a man caked in mud . . . who has to be coaxed into working with the promise of a dead fish. To the audience's delighted disgust, he bites off the fish's head and spits it into the crowd' (*Mail on Sunday*, 4 June). The way he was treated at the end of the play confirmed the production's essentially benevolent approach: 'deep down, there's something human, hungry and acquisitive about this creature, which Prospero recognizes and responds to in his parting gesture when he lets him keep his hat, and what's more, shows him how to wear it like a gentleman. A warm and touching benediction.' In the case of Ariel, the Globe setting was used to great advantage: 'Geraldine Alexander's Ariel, granted her freedom at last, did not fly off but slid down into the courtyard and walked off, entranced, through the crowd' (Paul Taylor, *Independent*, 30 May).

The Tempest returned to Shakespeare's Globe in 2005 with Mark Rylance, the outgoing artistic director, as Prospero. In a three-person cast he also played Alonso, Sebastian and Stephano, as well as emulating Gielgud in *Prospero's Books* by speaking the whole of the first scene. Alex Hassell played Caliban, Ferdinand and Gonzalo, Edward Hogg Miranda, Ariel, and Trinculo and Antonio. Some of the doubling emphasized links between characters (Caliban and Ferdinand as Miranda's suitors, Ariel and Miranda as quasi-sisters, Prospero and Alonso as rulers) and in the programme the director Tim Carroll stressed both the idea that the play takes place in Prospero's mind and ideas about psychological repression. This production then drew on thoughts that Ariel, Caliban and Prospero had some allegorical or psychological significance in terms of representing different aspects of the psyche, the idea that the physical and vocal dexterity of the performers could in some ways encapsulate the magic of the island and, showing the persistence of biographical interpretations, the suggestion that the play could stage both Shakespeare's farewell to his art and Rylance's farewell to the Globe.

5 *The Play on Screen*

The relationship between *The Tempest* and the medium of film has been characterized by an emphasis on the potential of new technologies to realize magic with spectacular effect, from the earliest extant (silent) film of *The Tempest*, dating from 1908, to the computer technology deployed in *Prospero's Books* (1991). The 1908 film exploits a mixture of theatrical and cinematic special effects to convey the magic of the play: the shipwreck involves a model boat capsizing, seen through a hole cut in a cloth in a style reminiscent of that used by many stage directors in both the nineteenth and twentieth centuries. The director is able to use the camera to present Ariel as both present and absent, presumably by stopping the camera and getting the actor to move in and out of shot as required. In this film we also see Prospero and Miranda before the ship sinks, with Prospero creating the storm via a cauldron, thus initiating the filmic tendency to open out the play to include aspects of its back-story and scenes that Shakespeare himself did not dramatize (the film was recently released on *Silent Shakespeare*). Other silent versions are lost and there appears to have been little interest in the play as a potential film over subsequent decades.

The majority of film treatments of *The Tempest* have been adaptations. The western *The Yellow Sky* (William Wellman, 1949) echoes the play to some extent:

> A band of bank robbers on the run from a posse flee into the desert. Near death from lack of water they stumble into what appears to be a ghost town, only to discover an old prospector and his granddaughter living there. The robbers discover that the old man has been mining gold and set out to make a quick fortune by robbing the pair. Their plan runs foul when the gang leader, Stretch (Gregory Peck), falls for the granddaughter (Anne Baxter), which sets off a showdown between the entire gang.   (DesMarais)

A striking response to the play in the science fiction film *Forbidden Planet* (Fred M. Wilcox, 1956) was followed towards the end of the century by three very different versions: Derek Jarman's 'punk' *The Tempest* (1980), Paul Mazursky's updated *Tempest* (1982), and Peter Greenway's prismatic *Prospero's Books* (1991).

In *Forbidden Planet* Caliban manifests himself as a monster from Prospero's id, adapting Shakespeare to a pop Freudian psychology that itself links back to some earlier critical attempts to schematize Prospero, Ariel and Caliban in terms that approximate to 'superego', 'ego' and 'id'. The Prospero figure, Doctor Morbius (Walter Pidgeon), has been trapped with his daughter Altaira (Anne Francis) on Altair IV after the crash of their spaceship, and the deaths of the rest of the crew at the hands of the monster, which eventually turns out to be the product of Morbius's id. Morbius, like Prospero, has access to arcane knowledge – in his case the scientific secrets of an ancient alien race. A rescue mission, led by a wooden Leslie Nielsen (as Commander Adams), arrives; Altaira falls in love with him, echoing the Ferdinand–Miranda plot, and the ship's cook forms a relationship with Robby the Robot, Prospero's servant (who combines facets of both Ariel and Caliban) that faintly echoes some aspects of the Caliban–Stephano–Trinculo plot. Morbius's pursuit of knowledge blinds him to the consequences of his actions and he is eventually destroyed along with the planet as Altaira escapes with Adams. The film in turn inspired Bob Carlton's theatrical parody rock opera *Return to the Forbidden Planet* (1989), which draws on the film, the source play and other plays by Shakespeare as well as a library of popular songs. In this case the lonely planet is D'Illyria, the rescuer is Captain Tempest, Miranda is the beautiful heroine and Ariel adds roller skating to his accomplishments. If *The Yellow Sky* and, to some extent, *Forbidden Planet* explore revenge tragedy – one of the play's potential generic configurations – more than the play itself, it is also noteworthy that Prospero himself becomes a much more complex and even evil character: there is no doubt in *Forbidden Planet* that Morbius's hubris causes his downfall and that he is seen as a Faustian figure who crosses the line from legitimate scientific curiosity into something much more like megalomania.

Whereas *Forbidden Planet* and later Mazursky's *Tempest* used situational parallels and elements of the story of *The Tempest*, neither used

Shakespeare's language, but both Jarman and Greenaway did. One of the characteristics of Jarman's and Greenaway's films is that each gives specific coverage to aspects of the prehistory of some of the relationships, showing elements of the story unstaged by Shakespeare. In his 1980 version, Jarman shows us Sycorax, Caliban and Ariel before Ariel was imprisoned in the pine, with Ariel refusing to suckle at Sycorax's breast, and Miranda sees herself at court. He also attacked the problem of the play's longer expository speeches by fragmenting speeches and, in the nobles' case, whole scenes. Jarman cast Heathcote Williams as his Prospero, establishing him as younger than the grandfatherly figure familiar from an older stage tradition, while his Miranda was Toyah Wilcox, then better known as a rock star. Much of the play took place in a dilapidated mansion and the boundaries between dream and reality were not always clear. Ariel was played by Karl Johnson in a white boiler suit, and Caliban (Jack Birkett) cracking and sucking a raw egg worked well in establishing his bestial nature. Jarman's film includes many interesting moments: Sebastian is a cleric, Ferdinand and Caliban work together on the log piling, Ariel sings part of a masque to Miranda, who knows he's there; Prospero and Caliban pronounce Sycorax differently; and at one point Prospero crushes Caliban's fingers. Perhaps the most startling innovation is the treatment of the masque, which takes the form of a dance by some of the campest sailors ever screened, followed by the Blues diva Elizabeth Welch singing 'Stormy Weather'. Obviously Jarman's treatment is not particularly 'faithful' to Shakespeare's play in many respects and it is open to criticism that, for example, Miranda seems too old and that her relationship with Caliban is one of amused tolerance rather than fear, but overall the film seems to have qualities of 'strangeness' that do some justice to many elements of Shakespeare's work.

Paul Mazursky's updated *Tempest* (1982) jettisons Shakespeare's language completely but is replete with echoes of his themes and his situations. As Mazursky wrote: 'The big decision was to move the storm from the beginning of the movie to the eighty percent point. Shakespeare starts with the storm. In my opinion, by starting with the storm you have nowhere to go. It's too big' (Taylor, p. 8). Certainly this is a problem that many stage productions have suffered from and Mazursky's decision allows him to explore many aspects of the issues that Shakespeare chooses not to concentrate on. However, what he does concentrate on is a tale of mid-life crisis with essentially domestic ramifications rather than the rather grander Shakespearean sweep of political thought, government and dynastic marriage. In the film, Philip, a New York architect (John Cassavetes), tires of metropolitan life and retreats to a Greek island peopled originally only by Kalibanos (Raul Julia) and his goats, taking with him a newly acquired mistress (Susan Sarandon) and his adolescent daughter Miranda (Molly Ringwald). Mazursky's version stages many scenes only hinted at by Shakespeare, for example Kalibanos spying on a naked Miranda swimming. Some Shakespearean characters change gender, so that Antonia's (Gena Rowlands) betrayal is in having an affair with Philip's boss Alonso (Vittorio Gassman), partly as a result of Philip's increasing introversion as his mid-life crisis develops. Eventually all the characters meet again on Philip's island after a huge storm, and are reconciled. Mazursky wrote that 'what appealed to me about the play was the plot: A man and his daughter on an island. A man consumed with negative feelings about his past. A man who felt that terrible things had been done to him and who in the end would put down his magic and forgive.'

The major elements of Peter Greenaway's *Prospero's Books* (1991) are a visual exploration of the kinds of books that Gonzalo might have provided Prospero with and how they might have helped him, using a variety of state-of-the-art computer techniques, and John Gielgud as Prospero, not only reprising a role he had played on stage several times over more than sixty years, but speaking the majority of the play's lines until, very late in the film, the other characters find their own voices. As Greenaway put it,

> [Prospero] invents characters to flesh out his imaginary fantasy to steer his enemies into his power, writes their dialogue, and having written it, he speaks the lines aloud, shaping the characters so powerfully through the words that they are conjured before us. . . . The characters walk and gesture, act and react, but still they do not speak. . . . They continue to be the mouthpiece of Prospero, the master dramatist. And this is the way things remain for as long as *The Tempest* is guided by the traditions of the revenge tragedy. . . . When his enemies are totally in his power, Prospero

is admonished by Ariel for the ferocity of the revengeful humiliation he forces on them, and he repudiates his plans and turns instead to forgiveness. The characters that his passion for revenge had created out of words now speak for the first time with their own voices, brought to a full life by his act of compassion.   (Greenaway, p. 9)

Among many interesting aspects of Greenaway's treatment of Shakespeare was his decision to emphasize the four elements (air, earth, fire and water), the use of multiple Ariels and his decision to have Caliban played by the naked dancer Michael Clark, which meant that Caliban's deformity was a matter of words rather than his actual physical appearance. Greenaway also adopted an approach similar to that of Jarman and Mazursky in presenting parts of the prehistory of the play and offering visual glosses on specific passages. The film features many of the characters who are spoken of but do not appear in Shakespeare's play: we see Sycorax and the birth of Caliban, Ariel confined in the pine, scenes of pre-revolutionary Milan (with Prospero's wife), Alonso and Antonio's coup d'état (with the sack of Milan and dead bodies), Caliban and Miranda as children together, the betrothal of Claribel to the black Prince of Tunis and the bloody aftermath of her defloration. While, in other *Tempest* films, showing some aspects of the pre-story reduces some of the problems of the play's notoriously difficult exposition, in *Prospero's Books* Greenaway's painterly vision extends into a somewhat indigestible feast of exposition in which the illustration of context and the use of visual allusion sometimes threatens to swamp the Shakespearean text. In many ways the film's vision of the play is remarkably old-fashioned: the richness of the illustrative material recalls in some ways the pedantically spectacular archaeologizing of Charles Kean, or Beerbohm Tree's defence of his spectacular approach by saying that Shakespeare would have wanted to utilize the most modern techniques of stagecraft available to him, just as Tree did. Greenaway also pursued the old idea of identification between Shakespeare's supposed farewell to his art and Prospero's giving up magic, and he wrote explicitly of an attempt to foster an equation between Prospero, Shakespeare and Gielgud. Throughout the film, as Gielgud voices the words of the play and apparently writes them down we are encouraged to develop this equation for ourselves until, at the end, when the books are drowned they include an incomplete First Folio, still awaiting *The Tempest*, and the newly completed *Tempest* itself. Ironically both are rescued from the water by Caliban.

There have been a number of made-for-television versions of *The Tempest*, sometimes with starry casts, but alongside these more or less faithful versions there have been other works that bounce off the play in some respects. *The Tempest* features in *Star Trek the Next Generation* in an episode called *Emergence*, in which Data the android is rehearsing as Prospero; while the series *Lost* appears to at the least draw on motifs associated with *The Tempest*: a wreck on a remote island (a plane rather than a ship), miraculous survivals, strange goings on in the interior, problems with water, visions and threats, and rebellions against leaders are some of the familiar ingredients that demonstrate the perennial appeal of the ingredients Shakespeare used. In the Norwegian animated film *Resan till Melonia* (1989, scripted by Per Åhlin and Karl Rasmusson, directed by Åhlin), apparently, 'The beautiful paradise island Melonia is inhabited by the wizard Prospero, his daughter Miranda and all their friends. The island is under threat from the coal black industry island Plutonia, governed by two profit hungry managers who keeps [sic] small children as their slaves in the factories' (Mattias Thuresson, www.imdb.com/title/tt0098189/plotsummary; downloaded 10 February 2005).

6 Critical Assessments

As well as dealing with conventional critical responses to the play, this section is a very highly selective account of some of the ways the play has inspired other creative works and played a role in wider political and commercial discourses. Like many plays, *The Tempest* has inspired numerous paintings, settings of music and sculptures that in some way relate to Shakespeare's original work. It has been produced in a wide variety of different ways ranging from the faithful to the deconstructed and has been filmed for cinema and television from widely differing viewpoints. (Some of the most significant versions are discussed in Chapter 4, 'Key Productions and Performances' and Chapter 5, 'The Play on Screen'.) However, the play has also found itself used in a very wide variety of discourses outside those of the arts: in South America Ariel and Caliban have a rich cultural and political life that extends over many decades and many countries; in political discourse in Britain Caliban can still be used to call up the bogey man in the same kinds of ways that he was in nineteenth-century *Punch* cartoons of the Irish as Caliban.

The seventeenth and eighteenth centuries

Even before Dryden and Davenant created their adaptation in 1667, *The Tempest* had influenced John Fletcher's *The Sea Voyage* (1622), John Milton's *Comus* (1634) and John Suckling's *The Goblins* (1638). Although Caliban is a relatively minor character in terms of the number of lines he speaks, the scenes he appears in, and the number of lines that are addressed to him or refer to him, he has exerted a powerful pull on the imagination of subsequent commentators. From Ben Jonson's brief strictures in the Induction to *Bartholomew Fair* onwards (see Chapter 3, 'The Play's Sources and Cultural Context'), early criticism of *The Tempest* was dominated by interest in Caliban and how Shakespeare had somehow managed to create a creature who did not exist in nature but yet spoke a language that matched neo-classical ideas of decorum by being just the kind of language that such a creature might have been expected to speak had it existed. Although this seems a largely circular argument, it was useful in developing a picture of a Shakespeare who could be defended against the more rigid neo-classicists.

As well as adapting Shakespeare's play with Davenant in 1667, Dryden appears to have been the first to write at any length on Caliban:

> He seems there to have created a person which was not in nature, a bold-ness which, at first sight, would appear intolerable; for he makes him a species of himself, begotten by an incubus on a witch. . . . Whether or no his generation can be defended, I leave to philosophy; but of this I am certain, that the poet has most judiciously furnished him with a person, a language and a character, which will suit him, both by father's and mother's side: he has all the discontents, and malice of a witch, and of a devil besides a convenient proportion of the deadly sins; gluttony, sloth and lust, are manifest; the dejectedness of a slave is likewise given him, and the ignorance of one bred up in a desert island. His person is monstrous, as he is the product of unnatural lust; and his language is as hobgoblin as his person; in all things he is distinguished from other mortals.   (Preface to *Troilus and Cressida*, London, 1679)

Dryden was followed by Nicholas Rowe, who prefaced his 1709 edition of Shakespeare's works with an essay that was highly influ-ential and established parameters that were followed by many subse-quent critics, biographers and editors, partly because it was often reproduced in subsequent editions, not always with acknowledge-ments of its provenance. It is, therefore, worth quoting Rowe's views at some length as they established much of the eighteenth century's critical agenda for *The Tempest*:

> certainly the greatness of this author's genius does nowhere so much appear, as where he gives his imagination an entire loose, and raises his

fancy to a flight above mankind and the limits of the visible world. Such are his attempts in The Tempest, Midsummer-Night's Dream, Macbeth and Hamlet. Of these, The Tempest, however it comes to be placed the first by the former publishers of his works, can never have been the first written by him: it seems to me as perfect in its kind, as almost any thing we have of his. One may observe, that the unities are kept here with an exactness uncommon to the liberties of his writing: though that was what, I suppose, he valued himself least upon, since his excellencies were all of another kind. I am very sensible that he does, in this play, depart too much from that likeness to truth which ought to be observed in these sort of writings; yet he does it so very finely, that one is easily drawn in to have more faith for his sake, than reason does well allow of. His magic has something in it very solemn and very poetical: and that extravagant character of Caliban is mighty well sustained, shows a wonderful invention in the author, who could strike out such a particular wild image, and is certainly one of the finest and most uncommon grotesques that was ever seen. The observation, which I have been informed three very great men [Rowe's note: Lord Falkland, Lord C. J. Vaughan and Mr. Selden] concurred in making upon this part, was extremely just. That Shakespeare had not only found out a new character in his Caliban but had also devised and adapted a new manner of language for that character. Among the particular beauties of this piece, I think one may be allowed to point out the tale of Prospero in the first act; his speech to Ferdinand in the fourth, upon the breaking up the masque of Juno and Ceres; and that in the fifth, where he dissolves his charms, and resolves to break his magic rod. (Nicholas Rowe, *Some Account of the Life &c of Mr William Shakespear*, London, 1709)

Rowe's emphasis on Caliban, Shakespeare's observation of the unities, and the 'beauties' of the play was picked up by writers like the influential critic Joseph Warton, who anticipated the Romantic emphasis on the importance of imagination and emphasized that Shakespeare's genius allowed him to transcend the neo-classical rules that he believed bound lesser authors:

As Shakespeare is sometimes blameable for the conduct of his fables, which have no unity; and sometimes for his diction, which is obscure and turgid; so his characteristical excellencies may possibly be reduced to these three general heads: his lively creative imagination; his strokes of

nature and passion; and his preservation of the consistency of his characters. These excellencies, particularly the last, are of so much importance
in the drama, that they amply compensate for his transgressions against
the rules of Time and Place, which being of a more mechanical nature, are
often strictly observed by a genius of the lowest order; but to portray
characters naturally, and to preserve them uniformly, requires such an
intimate knowledge of the heart of man, and is so rare a portion of felic-
ity, as to have been enjoyed, perhaps, only by two writers, Homer and
Shakespeare.

Of all the plays of Shakespeare, The Tempest is the most striking
instance of his creative power. He has there given the reins to his boundless
imagination, and has carried the romantic, the wonderful, and the wild, to
the most pleasing extravagance.   (The Adventurer, 93, London, 1753)

Throughout the eighteenth century Shakespeare's version of *The
Tempest* and adaptations deriving from the Dryden/Davenant version
of 1667 co-existed in different media. On the one hand, Shakespeare's
play was essentially something to be read and admired along the
lines established by Dryden's and Rowe's criticism, and Alexander
Pope's edition went so far as to highlight the best lines and relegate
the ones he disapproved of to the bottom of the page. On the other
hand, the theatrical public saw a succession of largely un-
Shakespearean versions, and the situation is neatly summed up in the
many collections of noteworthy quotations published during the
period, under such headings as *The Beauties of the English Stage* (1737), in
which the selected highlights of both plays might be granted a place.
At the end of the century, Francis Godolphin Waldron's play *The
Virgin Queen* (1797) addressed some of the questions about the ending
of the original that have concerned later critics: Caliban, Antonio and
Sebastian get together on the voyage back to Italy in a rather more
effective coup than they managed on the island and the situation is
only saved when Ariel recovers Prospero's staff and book.

Romantic and Victorian responses

As one might expect, Romantic critics were generally impressed by
the play as literature and particularly enthusiastic about some

speeches, but doubtful about its stage worthiness, and they had no opportunity to see it staged in anything like its original state until Macready's production in 1838. Coleridge emphasized that the play 'addresses itself entirely to the imaginative faculty; . . . the principal and only genuine excitement ought to come from within'. To him it was 'a specimen of the romantic drama; i.e. of a drama the interests of which are independent of all historical facts and associations, and arise from their fitness to that faculty of our nature, the imagination I mean, which gives no allegiance to time and place' (in Terence Hawkes (ed.), *Coleridge on Shakespeare*, Harmondsworth, 1969, p. 224). William Hazlitt saw something similar, still exploring along lines largely suggested by Dryden and Rowe:

> The human and imaginary characters, the dramatic and the grotesque, are blended together with the greatest art, and without any appearance of it. Though he has here given 'to airy nothing a local habitation and a name', yet that part which is only the fantastic creation of his mind, has the same palpable texture, and coheres 'semblably' with the rest. As the preternatural part has the air of reality, and almost haunts the imagination with a sense of truth, the real characters and events partake of the wildness of a dream.   (William Hazlitt, *The Characters of Shakespear's Plays*, London, 1817)

Both Coleridge and Hazlitt were interested in the contrasts between Caliban and Ariel, while Percy Bysshe Shelley envisaged himself as Ariel speaking to Miranda, in 'With a Guitar, to Jane' (1832). Following Thomas Campbell's suggestion in 1838 that Prospero was a self-portrait by Shakespeare, the way was open for increasingly allegorical readings of the play, in which Prospero, Caliban, Ariel and sometimes Miranda were to take their places in a kaleidoscopic set of variations on some themes from Shakespeare that would reach its apogee in the late nineteenth century. For example, Robert Browning's *Caliban upon Setebos* (1864) is a monologue in which Caliban is imagined trying to think through some theological conundrums about his mother's god.

In 1808 Edmund Malone had been the first to draw attention to the importance of the Bermuda pamphlets to the genesis of the play in colonial enterprises, and popular discourse quickly picked up on the theme of Caliban as a slave, a black man, a proletarian or an

Irishman (in newspaper cartoons, theatrical burlesques, periodical essays and occasional responses to theatrical interpretations). Charlotte Barnes's *The Forest Princess* (1844) combined *The Tempest* with the story of Pocahontas, a reminder of how close Shakespeare himself came to dramatizing another potent colonial theme. Later in the century there was also interest in *The Tempest* in terms of the evolution controversy and the idea of Caliban as a Darwinian missing link between the apes and humanity, when Daniel Wilson suggested that Shakespeare had anticipated Darwin: 'The not wholly irrational brute, the animal approximating in form and attributes as nearly to man as the lower animal may be supposed to do while still remaining a brute, has actually been conceived for us . . . in one of the most original creations of the Shakespearean drama' (*Caliban: The Missing Link*, London, 1873, p. 9).

In 1875 Edward Dowden usefully summarized some of the main allegorical strands of the period:

> Caliban, says Kreyssig, is the People. He is Understanding apart from Imagination, declares Professor Lowell. He is the primitive man abandoned to himself, declares M. Mézières; Shakespeare would say to Utopian thinkers, predecessors of Jean Jacques Rousseau, 'Your hero walks on four feet as well as on two.' . . . Caliban is one of the powers of nature over which the scientific intellect obtains command, another critic assures us, and Prospero is the founder of the Inductive Philosophy. Caliban is the colony of Virginia. Caliban is the untutored early drama of Marlowe. (*Shakspere: A Critical Study of his Mind and Art*, 12th edn, London, 1901, p. 424)

The title of Dowden's study, *Shakspere: A Critical Study of his Mind and Art*, is indicative of how, following the Romantics, late nineteenth-century critics tended to read the plays in terms of a psycho-biography that could be recovered from the texts. Dowden divided Shakespeare's life and work into four periods: 'In the Workshop', 'In the World', 'Out of the Depths' and 'On the Heights', which is the period of *The Tempest*. Dowden's work was enormously influential (and contains some astute criticism) but it furthered the identification of Shakespeare and Prospero and, despite some comments in which he drew attention to Prospero's internal struggles, the idea of both Shakespeare's and Prospero's untroubled serenity:

It is not chiefly because Prospero is a great enchanter, now about to break his magic staff, to drown his book deeper than ever plummet sounded, to dismiss his airy spirits, and to return to the practical service of his Dukedom, that we identify Prospero in some measure with Shakspere himself. It is rather because the temper of Prospero, the grave harmony of his character, his self-mastery, his calm validity of will, his sensitiveness to wrong, his unfaltering justice, and with these, a certain abandonment, a remoteness from the common joys and sorrows of the world, are characteristic of Shakspere as discovered to us in all his latest plays. (*Shakspere: A Critical Study of his Mind and Art*, p. 417)

This judgement neatly encapsulated a dominant orthodoxy in which the equation of Prospero with Shakespeare and of both with the serene wisdom of advancing age was reflected both on stage and in critical assessments of the play. Such views drew an angry riposte from the iconoclastic Lytton Strachey, who countered that:

It is difficult to resist the conclusion that he [Shakespeare] was getting bored himself. Bored with people, bored with real life, bored with drama, bored, in fact, with everything except poetry and poetical dreams . . . on the one side inspired by a soaring fancy to the singing of ethereal songs, and on the other urged by a general disgust to burst occasionally through his torpor into bitter and violent speech? If we are to learn anything of his mind from his last works, it is surely this.

In The Tempest, unreality has reached its apotheosis. Two of the principal characters are frankly not human beings at all; and the whole action passes, through a series of impossible occurrences, in a place which can only by courtesy be said to exist. The Enchanted Island, indeed, peopled, for a timeless moment, by this strange fantastic medley of persons and of things, has been cut adrift for ever from common sense, and floats, buoyed up by a sea, not of waters, but of poetry. ('Shakespeare's Final Period', originally 1906, in *Books and Characters French and English*, London, 1922)

Strachey was given valiant support by E. E. Stoll, who tried to dismiss allegorical readings by insisting that:

That the story is slight is no proof that there is another within or behind it. And Prospero is not Shakespeare any more than (as fewer think) he is

James I, except in the sense that the dramatist, not the Scotch monarch, created him; his 'potent art' of magic is not the art of poetry; Ariel is not genius, or the lawless imagination, craving liberty but kept in service; Miranda is not the drama; Caliban not the vulgar public; Milan not Stratford; and the enchanted isle not the stage, or London, or the world. (E. E. Stoll, originally 1927, in *Art and Artifice*, London, 1963).

However, neither Strachey nor Stoll could stem the tide of biographical and allegorical readings, which continued (and continues today) to influence both readings and stagings of the play. Although some of these readings are highly speculative and convoluted in their attempts to fit the play into unlikely matrices, the play itself, with its two supernatural characters under the control of a human being, and Prospero's two big speeches about the ephemeral nature of the theatre and his intention to give up magic, does provide fertile ground for such interpretations.

The twentieth century and beyond

With the growth of university courses in English and drama, the amount of literary and theatrical scholarship has increased massively and it becomes harder to do full justice to the range of views, although it is possible to pick out some significant strands. Anyone wanting to discover the state of the art in critical and scholarly approaches to *The Tempest* will find it useful to consult the latest issues of the well-established journal *Shakespeare Quarterly* and the annual *Shakespeare Survey* and will find two volumes by Alden and Virginia Vaughan, and Hulme and Sherman's *'The Tempest' and Its Travels*, full of important insights into the critical, scholarly, and theatrical fortunes of the play.

Two of the most influential early twentieth-century Shakespearean critics pursued approaches that resembled Dowden's. Both G. Wilson Knight in *Myth and Miracle* (1929) and E. M. W. Tillyard in *Shakespeare's Last Plays* (1938) saw the last plays as representing the culmination of a process of Shakespeare working through both moral and technical issues towards a new world in which tragic experiences can be converted into a new post-tragic synthesis. Although their criticism is subtle enough not to fall into the obvious biographical traps, both are interested in tracing the author's artistic development. Wilson Knight returned to *The Tempest* throughout his long career and one of his last essays 'Caliban as a Red Man' (1980), revisited many of his ideas, pursuing them through the character of Caliban in ways that straddle the eighteenth-century interest in Caliban's language, the nineteenth-century identification of Prospero and Shakespeare and even the New Historicist interest in the play's colonial contexts.

Much eighteenth- and nineteenth-century criticism had drawn attention to the noteworthy qualities of particular passages of the play but it seldom went beyond noting those qualities and exhorting readers to enjoy them. The early twentieth-century interest in 'Practical Criticism' led to some very detailed readings of how the play's poetry actually worked, including Wilson Knight's, but Reuben A. Brower's extended discussion (1951) is amongst the finest. Brower demonstrates with great clarity and perception that:

> The harmony of the play lies in its metaphorical design, in the closeness and completeness with which its rich and varied elements are linked through almost inexhaustible analogies. It is hard to pick a speech at random without coming on an expression that brings us by analogy into direct contact with elements that seem remote . . . he makes use of a few fairly constant analogies that can be traced through expressions sometimes the same and sometimes extraordinarily varied. And the recurrent analogies (or continuities) are linked through a key metaphor into a single metaphorical design. . . . The surest proof of the pervasiveness of Shakespearean design lies in the mere number of continuities that can be discovered in the play. But some are more important than others because they can be traced through more expressions or in more scenes and because they express analogies more closely related to the key metaphor. The six main continuities, roughly labeled to indicate their character, are: 'strange-wondrous', 'sleep-and-dream', 'sea-tempest', 'music-and-noise', 'earth-air', 'slavery-freedom', and 'sovereignty-conspiracy'. (In D. J. Palmer (ed.), *Shakespeare: The Tempest*, London: Macmillan Casebook Series, 1991, pp. 131–3)

There has been considerable interest in the genre of *The Tempest*, much of which is reflected in my discussion of its 'Sources and Cultural Context' (see Chapter 3) and much of which is usefully summarized in a number of important one-volume editions from the last half-century. Frank Kermode's erudite and illuminating Arden edition, of 1954, places great emphasis on the opposition 'between the worlds of Prospero's Art and Caliban's Nature', in which Caliban represents 'nature without benefit of nurture', as opposed to 'Prospero's benevolent Art' (pp. xxiv–xxv). So great was this edition's influence that it has become a target of post-colonial critics, who sometimes erect it as a straw man to target for not being concerned enough with the politics of the play. Anne (Righter) Barton's excellent but rather neglected introduction to the New Penguin Shakespeare edition (1968) offers a persuasive reading, closely based in the text of the play, that follows Brower in showing the importance of being alert to the subtleties and nuances of the way the play actually uses language. Northrop Frye's extended engagement with Shakespeare's work as he developed his archetypal criticism offered persuasive readings of *The Tempest* that avoided the pitfalls of overextended allegorical criticism in *The Anatomy of Criticism* (1957), *A Natural Perspective* (1965) and in his 1959 Pelican edition of the play. Undoubtedly, contemporary critical interest has widened to include much more consideration of both colonial issues and the play in the theatre than was usual when Kermode, Frye and Barton prepared their editions. Stephen Orgel effortlessly synthesizes his own work on the masque, New Historical readings and theatre-based criticism to produce a wide-ranging account of the play in his Oxford edition (1987). The fullest account of *The Tempest* in the theatre is Christine Dymkowski's 'Plays in Performance' edition, which includes a lengthy historical account of the play's fortunes and line-by-line annotations of significant interpretations (2000).

Recent scholarship has tended to focus on the themes of slavery, colonialism and government in thorough explorations of the historical factors that informed the period of the creation of the play, including many aspects of the relationships between the Americas, the Mediterranean and England, including the slave trade. Sidney Lee's 1898 biography of Shakespeare was probably the first serious academic work to suggest that *The Tempest* was 'a veritable document of early Anglo-American history' (p. 257) and he was followed by writers like Leo Marx, who saw *The Tempest* as Shakespeare's

'American Fable' because its concern with Pastoral could be linked to the ways in which colonists reacted to the untamed lands of the Americas, and like Leslie Fiedler in *The Stranger in Shakespeare* (see Hulme and Sherman, p. 172).

Stephen Greenblatt's essay 'Learning to Curse' (1976) was one of the earliest and most influential academic readings in recent times, effectively inaugurating the New Historicist work on *The Tempest*, which has become a critical orthodoxy against which there has been some reaction in recent years, simply because there is an occasionally reductive tendency, in some of the many attempts to read the play in terms of its historical contexts, to reduce it to no more than a convenient document illustrating colonial themes. In 1989 Meredith Skura provided an important corrective to some of the more grandiose claims of New Historicist criticism of *The Tempest*. However, alongside the interesting examples of works that have explored the colonial issues with reference to slavery and the New World, some New Historicists and British Cultural Materialists have looked at social conflicts in Jacobean England through the stereotyping of people on the margins of society and attempts to dramatize some immediately compelling debates about social organization. Similarly critical explorations of English colonialism in Ireland have shown how *The Tempest* and particularly the figure of Caliban can be directly related to plantations much nearer to home than the West Indies, and serve as a useful reminder that the demonization of the Irish as Calibans in nineteenth-century *Punch* cartoons may relate more directly to the play's original conceptual basis than has sometimes been allowed by those who are sceptical of modern trends in criticism. (See Hulme and Sherman for examples and further references.)

Many novels have taken up themes from *The Tempest*. The most famous, Aldous Huxley's *Brave New World* (1932), takes its title from Miranda's response to the Italian noblemen but envisages a dystopian world in which genetic engineering has produced a society without freedoms. The outsider here is John, who is seen as 'savage' because he has come from outside 'civilization' but, unlike Miranda, he is appalled by what he sees. Canadian author Robertson Davies's *Tempest-Tost* (1951) is a novel about an amateur company staging *The Tempest*. Isak Dinesen (Karen Blixen)'s story *Tempest* from *Anecdotes of*

Destiny (1958) derives from Shakespeare, and John Fowles also uses elements from *The Tempest* in *The Magus* (1965).

Despite the recent dominance of post-colonial critical readings, other strands of scholarship have, of course, continued. The traditional emphasis on the last plays as a group continued in Frances Yates's *Shakespeare's Last Plays: A New Approach* (1975) and *The Occult Philosophy in the Elizabethan Age* (1979). Yates, who was an expert on many arcane areas of Renaissance thought, saw Shakespeare's presentation of Prospero as being a defence of the magician John Dee, who was being malignly neglected by James I. Andrew Gurr has considered 'The Tempest's Tempest at Blackfriars' (1989), and a recent essay by Douglas Bruster has seen the play as dramatizing Renaissance theatre politics in ways that at times seem oddly reminiscent of Dowden or E. K. Chambers: Prospero is seen as the director/author, Miranda 'a figure of an idealized spectatorship' and Caliban an attack on Will Kemp ('a celebrated Elizabethan clown known for his physical, even priapic comedy, his independent spirit, folk ethos, and intrusive ad libs', who had in fact left the company some ten years before the play was first staged (quoted in Hulme and Sherman, p. 4).

Allegorical readings of *The Tempest* often see analogies between Prospero as a colonist and a representative of the ruling class and Caliban as colonized and a member of the proletariat, with Ariel sometimes regarded as a native who has been assimilated to European ways. Among the theatrical versions that have explored this dimension from radically different viewpoints are Beerbohm Tree's (1904) and Jonathan Miller's (1970) (see Chapter 4, 'Key Productions and Performances'). Unsurprisingly, intellectuals in former colonies have themselves tried to use the colonial elements in *The Tempest* in a variety of ways to understand their own situations. The Afro-Caribbean writer George Lamming, who addressed the colonial elements in *The Tempest* in his *The Pleasures Of Exile* (1960), identifying himself as a descendant of both the slave Caliban and his master Prospero, since he had been taught Prospero's language, subsequently published *Water With Berries* (1971), a novel whose title derived from one of Caliban's speeches, in which he inverts the experience of *The Tempest* to bring his Caribbeans to London. Marina

Warner's *Indigo* (1992) explores colonial themes, using *The Tempest* as her basis. Octave Mannoni used the relationship between Prospero and Caliban to explore the nature of a revolt in Madagascar in 1948 in his *Psychologie de la colonisation* (1950; published in English in 1956 as *Prospero and Caliban: The Psychology of Colonisation*). Mannoni himself had taught Aimé Césaire, author of *Une Tempête* (see Chapter 4, 'Key Productions and Performances').

As Gordon Brotherston has demonstrated, *The Tempest* (mediated in part through Ernest Renan's 1878 *Caliban, Suite de 'La Tempête'*, which followed Waldron in imagining events after Shakespeare's play) influenced philosophical and cultural debates in Latin America, and has played an important part in South America in crystallizing attitudes towards political issues over many decades, particularly those relating to the cultural and political hegemonies of Spain and the USA, even inspiring a political movement (*arielismo*) that in its turn influenced the British Labour politician Nye Bevan (Hulme and Sherman, pp. 212–19).

The best known poetic works using *The Tempest* often draw on either Ariel or Caliban, whereas W. H. Auden tries something even more ambitious in *The Sea and the Mirror* (1944), a mixture of prose and verse in which the play's characters are allowed to speak in a variety of different ways. Ironically Caliban is given a highly sophisticated and complex prose that presents him as a very different kind of person from Shakespeare's. Auden's Prospero is an artist renouncing his art, but both Caliban and Antonio represent a critique of the ways in which he has failed to control the world. Claribel figures large in H.D.'s *By Avon River* (1949), while it is perhaps not surprising that Sylvia Plath's engagement with *The Tempest* was called *Ariel* (1963) while her erstwhile husband Ted Hughes plumped for *Prospero and Sycorax* (1971).

Today the play continues to offer a sounding board for political ideas, as is amply attested by Silvia Federici's recent *Caliban and the Witch: Women, the Body and Primitive Accumulation*, in which:

> Caliban represents not only the anti-colonial rebel whose struggle still resonates in contemporary Caribbean literature, but is a symbol for the world proletariat and, more specifically, for the proletarian body as a

terrain and instrument of resistance to the logic of capitalism. Most important, the figure of the witch, who in *The Tempest* is confined to a remote background, in this volume is placed at the center-stage, as the embodiment of a world of female subjects that capitalism had to destroy: the heretic, the healer, the disobedient wife, the woman who dared to live alone, the obeha woman who poisoned the master's food and inspired the slaves to revolt.   (Autonomedia, Brooklyn, NY, 2004, p. 11)

Whether the name of the shop Caliban in Greifswalder Strasse, Berlin, that sells 'natural products' from South Asia refers directly to Shakespeare, to one of the post-colonial literary reworkings of *The Tempest*, or to one of the political appropriations of the character, is not entirely clear, but it is further proof of the pervasive resonances of Shakespeare's work some four centuries after it was written.

Further Reading

This annotated list of further reading includes both works cited and others that will enable the reader to pursue issues raised in the text. The modern editions of *The Tempest* listed below all include extensive detailed references. Some of the works may not be readily accessible in libraries or bookshops but there are a significant number of online editions of some of the older texts and many of the books are available through both 'bricks and mortar' or online second-hand bookshops.

Editions of *The Tempest*

Barton (Righter), Anne (ed.), *The Tempest*, New Penguin Shakespeare (Harmondsworth, 1968). A very useful edition with an excellent introduction that deals very effectively with the play's language.

Dymkowski, Christine (ed.), *The Tempest*, Shakespeare in Production (Cambridge, 2000). An excellent account of *The Tempest* in production, with accounts of how directors and actors have approached the play line by line.

Frye, Northrop (ed.), *The Tempest*, in *The Pelican Shakespeare* (Baltimore, MD, 1959). The introduction contains a useful expression of Frye's view of the play.

Kermode, Frank (ed.), *The Tempest*, Arden Shakespeare, 2nd series (London, 1954), revised and corrected 1961, 1962 (Arden 2). A very important edition that established a critical framework for many subsequent debates. Says little about the theatre or the colonial issues.

Orgel, Stephen (ed.), *The Tempest*, Oxford Shakespeare (Oxford, 1987). An excellent and comprehensive introduction dealing clearly with many important issues.

Vaughan, Virginia Mason, and Alden T. Vaughan (eds), *The Tempest*, Arden Shakespeare, 3rd series (London, 1999) (Arden 3). A recent edition, paying considerable attention to both colonial issues and the play in the theatre.

Collections of essays

Hulme, Peter, and William H. Sherman (eds), *'The Tempest' and Its Travels* (London, 2000). An extremely useful book with many fascinating and erudite essays on a wide range of topics, and a library of further reading in the notes. Introduces its readers to many complex issues, so best approached with some knowledge of the main themes of *Tempest* criticism.

Palmer, D. J. (ed.), *Shakespeare, 'The Tempest': A Casebook* (London, 1st edn, 1968; rev. edn, 1991). A useful collection of material including extracts from Dryden and Davenant's adaptation, criticism by Coleridge and Dowden, and twentieth-century critics. The revised edition includes material on colonial issues.

Vaughan, Virginia Mason, and Alden T. Vaughan (eds), *Critical Essays on Shakespeare's 'The Tempest'* (New York, 1998). A selection of significant recent essays that provides a good grounding in contemporary strands of interpretation of the play.

Theatre and film

Benson, Constance, *Mainly Players* (London, 1926). Reminiscences of F. R. Benson's company.

Booth, M. R. (ed.), *English Plays of the Nineteenth Century*, vol. V: *Pantomimes, Extravaganza and Burlesques* (Oxford, 1976). Reprints the script of William and Robert Brough's *The Enchanted Isle*.

Carlton, Bob, *Return to the Forbidden Planet* (London, 1985). The script of the rock opera inspired by *Forbidden Planet* and the works of Shakespeare.

Césaire, Aimé, *Une Tempête* (Paris, 1969). An influential modern adaptation of *The Tempest*.

Coursen, H. R., 'Two Versions of *The Tempest*', West Virginia Shakespeare and Renaissance Association Selected Papers, 20, 1997, www.marshall.edu/engsr//SR1997.html, downloaded 12 October 2005. Perceptive reviews of Patrick Stewart in George C. Wolfe's production and of one by Ron Daniels for the American Repertory Theatre.

DesMarais E.W. {jlongst@aol.com}www.imdb.com/title/tt0040978/ plotsummary, downloaded 10 February 2005. Plot summary of *Yellow Sky*.

Dryden, John, and William Davenant, *The Tempest* (London, 1670). The first adaptation of *The Tempest*.

Egan, Gabriel, 'Ariel's Costume in the Original Staging of *The Tempest*', *Theatre Notebook*, 51 (1997), 62–72. Includes important new information.

Foakes, R. A., and R. T. Rickert (eds), *Henslowe's Diary* (Cambridge, 1961). Philip Henslowe's papers offer an important insight into many aspects of how a Renaissance theatre company operated.

Gielgud, John, *An Actor and His Time* (London, 1979). Gives useful information on Gielgud's approach to Prospero in his various stage productions.

Gielgud, John, *Shakespeare – Hit or Miss?* (London, 1991). Contains useful information on Gielgud's approach to Prospero, including his work on *Prospero's Books*.

Greenaway, Peter, *Prospero's Books: A Film of Shakespeare's 'The Tempest'* (London, 1991). The book of the film, with an illuminating introduction by Greenaway and many illustrations.

Griffiths, Trevor R., ' "This Island's Mine": Caliban and Colonialism', *Yearbook of English Studies*, 13 (1983), 159–80. Theatrical responses to the play from the nineteenth and twentieth centuries, concentrating on colonial, republican and missing-link interpretations.

Gurr, Andrew, '*The Tempest*'s Tempest at Blackfriars', *Shakespeare Survey* 41 (1989), 91–102. A study of the likely conditions of early performances of the play.

Gurr, Andrew, *The Shakespearean Stage, 1574–1642*, 3rd edn (Cambridge, 1992). The standard work.

Hayman, Ronald, *John Gielgud* (London, 1971). Information on Gielgud's Prosperos to 1957.

Hirst, David L., *The Tempest: Text and Performance* (London, 1984). Useful readings of the play in performance.

Horowitz, Arthur, *Prospero's 'True Preservers'* (Newark, DE, 2004). Analysis of productions by Brook, Strehler and Ninagawa.

Marker, Frederick J., 'The First Night of Charles Kean's *The Tempest* – from the Notebook of Hans Christian Andersen', *Theatre Notebook*, 25 (1970), 20–3. The novelist's somewhat jaundiced responses to one of the nineteenth century's most spectacular productions.

Morley, Sheridan, *The Authorised Biography of John Gielgud* (London, 2001). Gielgud's Prosperos.

Osment, Philip, *This Island's Mine*, in *Gay Sweatshop: Four Plays and a Company*, intro. and ed., Philip Osment (London, 1989). Play about a modern production of *The Tempest*.

Shaw, Bernard, *Our Theatre in the Nineties* (London, 1932), vol. III.

Silent Shakespeare, British Film Institute videocassette and DVD (London, 1999). Includes the 1908 film of *The Tempest*.

Taylor, Geoffrey (ed.), *Paul Mazursky's 'Tempest'* (New York, NY, 1982). The book of the film.

The Tempest (London, 1839). Acting edition for Macready's production.

The Tempest as Arranged for the Stage by H. B. Tree (London, 1904). Tree's acting edition.

Thuresson, Mattias, www.imdb.com/title/tt0098189/plotsummary, downloaded 10 February 2005. Review of *Resan till Melonia*.

Trewin, J. C., *Benson and the Bensonians* (London, 1960). The standard work on F. R. Benson and his company.

Sources and contexts

Bate, Jonathan, *Shakespeare and Ovid* (Oxford, 1994). The standard modern work on Shakespeare's debt to Ovid.

Bullough, G. (ed.), *Narrative and Dramatic Sources of Shakespeare*, vol. VIII: *The Romances* (London, 1975). Still the standard work.

Day, Angel, *Daphnis and Chloe* (London, 1578). Translated from Jacques Amyot's French version of Longus.

Dod, John and Robert Cleaver, *A Godly Form of Household Government* (London, 1598).

Florio, John, *The Essays of Montaigne* (London, 1603).

Golding, Arthur (trans.), Ovid's *Metamorphoses* (London 1567).

Hughes, Jonathan, 'Base Matter into Gold', *History Today*, 55:8 (2005), 40–6. The life of a failed alchemist.

James VI of Scotland, *Basilicon Doron* (Edinburgh, 1599).

Jonson, Ben, *Hymenaei, or the Solemnities of a Masque and Barriers at a Marriage* (London, 1606).

Jonson, Ben, *Bartholomew Fair* (London, 1614).

Jourdain, Sylvester, *Discovery of the Barmudas* (London, 1610).

Rodger, N. A. M., *The Safeguard of the Sea* (Harmondsworth, 2004). Some illuminating material on maritime issues that contextualizes the first scene.

Sidney, Sir Philip, *Defence of Poesy* (London, 1595).

Strachey, William, *A true Repertory of the wrack and redemption of Sir Thomas Gates, Knight*, in Samuel Purchas, *Purchas His Pilgrims* (London, 1625).

Virginia Company, *A True Declaration of the state of the Colony in Virginia with a confutation of such scandalous reports as have tended to the disgrace of so worthy an enterprise* (London, 1610).

Critical assessments

Adventurer, The, 93 (1753). Joseph Warton on *The Tempest*.

Breight, Curt, ' "Treason doth never prosper": *The Tempest* and the Discourse of Treason', *Shakespeare Quarterly*, 41 (1990), 1–28. Examines the Jacobean social context of the play.

Brotherston, Gordon, '*Arielismo* and Anthropophagy: *The Tempest* in Latin America', in Peter Hulme and William H. Sherman (eds), *'The Tempest' and Its Travels* (London, 2000), pp. 212–19.

Brotton, Jerry, ' "This Tunis, sir, was Carthage": Contesting Colonialism', in Ania Loomba and Martin Orkin (eds), *Post-Colonial Shakespeares* (London, 1998).

Brower, Rueben A., *Fields of Light* (New York, NY, 1951). Includes a fine, extended, close reading of how language works in *The Tempest*.

Connor, John, *Shakespearean Afterlives: Ten Characters with a Life of their Own* (London, 2003). Includes a section on Prospero.

Dowden, Edward, *Shakspere: A Critical Study of his Mind and Art*, 12th edn (London, 1901). One of the major nineteenth-century works of Shakespeare criticism.

Dryden, John, Preface to *Troilus and Cressida* (London, 1679). Contains Dryden's views on Caliban.

Federici, Silvia, *Caliban and the Witch: Women, the Body and Primitive Accumulation* (Brooklyn, NY, 2004). An appropriation of Caliban for a modern feminist reading of aspects of social organization.

Felperin, Howard, *Shakespearian Romance* (Princeton, NJ, 1972). An important reading of the Romance genre as a whole, with discussion of Shakespeare's 'Romances'.

Fiedler, Leslie, *The Stranger in Shakespeare* (London, 1973). An important consideration of the role of outsiders in Shakespeare.

Frye, Northrop, *A Natural Perspective: The Development of Shakespearian Comedy and Romance* (New York, NY, 1965). Important accounts of the plays in terms of genre and myth.

Goss, John (ed.), *After Shakespeare: Writing Inspired by the World's Greatest Author* (Oxford, 2002). Responses to Shakespeare, some well known, some more obscure.

Greenblatt, Stephen, *'Learning to Curse': Essays in Early Modern Culture* (New York, NY, 1990). Reprints Greenblatt's pioneering New Historicist reading of the play.

Hawkes, Terence (ed.), *Coleridge on Shakespeare* (Harmondsworth, 1969). Includes Coleridge's responses to *The Tempest*.

Hazlitt, William, *The Characters of Shakespear's Plays* (London, 1817). Analysis of Caliban.

Knox, Bernard, 'The Tempest and the Ancient Comic Tradition', in W. K. Wimsatt (ed.), *English Stage Comedy* (New York, NY, 1955). Locates the play in the comic matrix of Plautine comedy with Prospero as the irritable old man (*senex*) and Ariel and Caliban as the slaves.

Lee, Sidney, *A Life of William Shakespeare* (London, 1898). Claims the play is a document of Anglo-American history.

Mannoni, Octave, *Prospero and Caliban: The Psychology of Colonization* (originally published in 1950 as *Psychologie de la Colonisation*), trans. Pamela Powesland (London, 1956). An important study of its subject that has been very influential in subsequent readings and stagings of *The Tempest*.

Marx, Leo, 'Shakespeare's American Fable', in *The Machine in the Garden: Technology and the Pastoral Ideal in America* (New York, NY, 1964). Originally published in 1960.

O'Connor, Marion, *William Poel and the Elizabethan Stage Society* (London, 1987).

Palmer, D. J. (ed.), *Shakespeare: The Tempest* (London: Macmillan, Casebook series, 1991).

Rowe, Nicholas, *Some Account of the Life &c of Mr William Shakespear* (London, 1709). The definitive eighteenth-century account of Shakespeare.

Skura, Meredith, 'Discourse and the Individual: the Case of Colonialism in *The Tempest*', *Shakespeare Quarterly*, 40 (1989), 42–69. A warning against over-concentration on colonial themes.

Stoll, E. E., *Art and Artifice* (London, 1963). Against allegorical readings of *The Tempest* (originally published in 1927).

Strachey, Lytton, *Books and Characters French and English* (London, 1922). Attack on bardolatry in relationship to *The Tempest*.

Styan, J. L., *The Shakespeare Revolution* (Cambridge, 1977). Important study of changes in approaches to Shakespeare at the turn of the nineteenth century.

Thomas, Keith, *Religion and the Decline of Magic* (London, 1971). An important study of ideas about magic.

Tillyard, E. M. W., *Shakespeare's Last Plays* (London, 1938).

Traversi, D., *Shakespeare: The Last Phase* (London, 1954).

Vaughan, Alden T., 'Trinculo's Indian: American Natives in Shakespeare's England', in Peter Hulme and William H. Sherman (eds), *'The Tempest' and Its Travels* (London, 2000), pp. 49–59.

Vaughan, Alden T. and Virginia Mason Vaughan, *Shakespeare's Caliban: A Cultural History* (Cambridge, 1991). An important survey.

Wilson, Daniel, *Caliban: The Missing Link* (London, 1873).

Wilson Knight, G., *Myth and Miracle* (London, 1929). *The Shakespearian Tempest* (Oxford, 1932) and *The Crown of Life: Essays in Interpretation of Shakespeare's Final Plays* (Oxford, 1947). Each includes studies of *The Tempest*.

Wilson Knight, G., 'Caliban as a Red Man', in Philip Edwards, Inga-Stina Ewbank and G. K. Hunter (eds), *Shakespeare's Styles: Essays in*

Honour of Kenneth Muir (Cambridge, 1980), pp. 205–20. Somewhat eccentric but indicative of Wilson Knight's highly eclectic approach to Shakespeare.

Yates, Frances, *Shakespeare's Last Plays: A New Approach* (London, 1975).

Yates, Frances, *The Occult Philosophy in the Elizabethan Age* (London, 1979).

Index